ALISON'S ADVENTURES

YOUR PASSPORT TO THE WORLD

Dedicated to my legendary explorer parents David Blehert and Deborah Koehn, thank you for giving me the world and inspiring my love to protect it.

Vice President, Licensing & Publishing	Amanda Joiner
Editorial Manager	Carrie Bolin
Editor	Jessica Firpi
Designer	Chris Conway
Contributors	Carrie Bolin, Engrid Barnett
Proofreader	Rachel Paul
Production Designer	Rose Audette
Reprographics	Bob Prohaska
Special Thanks to	John Graziano
Cover Artwork	Chris Conway

"*Educate through entertainment to make global impact.*"

Special Thanks to Alison Teal

Published by Ripley Publishing 2020

1 3 5 7 9 10 8 6 4 2

© Copyright 2020 by Alison's Adventures LLC

All rights reserved. Ripley's, Believe It or Not!, and Ripley's Believe It or Not! are registered trademarks of Ripley Entertainment Inc.

Named "THE FEMALE INDIANA JONES" by TIME Magazine From TIME. ©2015 TIME USA LLC. All rights reserved. Used under license.

ISBN 978-1-60991-337-3

Library of Congress Control Number: 2019956918

Manufactured in China in January 2020 by Leo Paper

First Printing

No part of this publication may be reproduced in whole or in part, stored in a retrieval system, or transmitted in any form by any means, electronic, mechanical, photocopying, recording, or otherwise, without written permission from the publisher.

www.penguin.co.uk

Young Arrow is part of the Penguin Random House group of companies whose addresses can be found at global.penguinrandomhouse.com

A CIP catalogue record for this book is available from the British Library

UK ISBN 978-1-52912-019-6

For more information regarding permission, contact:

VP Licensing & Publishing
Ripley Entertainment Inc.
7576 Kingspointe Parkway, Suite 188
Orlando, Florida 32819
publishing@ripleys.com
www.ripleys.com/books

PUBLISHER'S NOTE
While every effort has been made to verify the accuracy of the entries in this book, the Publisher cannot be held responsible for any errors contained in the work. They would be glad to receive any information from readers.

WARNING
Some of the stunts and activities are undertaken by experts and should not be attempted by anyone without adequate training and supervision.

ALISON'S ADVENTURES

YOUR PASSPORT TO THE WORLD

Ripley
PUBLISHING

a Jim Pattison Company

CONTENTS

Aloha, adventurers, and welcome to my book! I'm thrilled that I can share my life, my stories, and my work with you, the trailblazing reader. Since you've cracked open this coconut, I assume you might know a little about me, but just in case—

My name is Alison Teal, and I'm an explorer, survivalist, surfer, and filmmaker. I grew up homeschooled all around the world by my wild and daring adventurer photographer parents, so my childhood was pretty crazy. Traveling on the back of a camel or doing schoolwork on the flanks of Mount Everest—my parents raised me in the most primitive, exotic, and even dangerous places on Earth.

Eventually, we set up base camp in Hawaii, where over my lifetime my parents built a home by hand on this remote, pristine oceanfront paradise. Decades later, this true labor of love, our very own "Robinson Crusoe-style" grass shack, has evolved into a renowned retreat center and my beloved home. We live sustainably and teach others how to preserve our most valuable resource—our environment.

After graduating from film school, I decided to combine my love for filmmaking, acting, and exploration and create a new media storytelling series called *Alison's Adventures* to share my experiences with you—yes, you!—through films, photos, and even inspirational speaking.

And now, like a female version of Indiana Jones (except with a camera and my pink surfboard made from recycled coffee cups), I journey into ancient cultures seeking out the greatest myths, mysteries, and legends, not to mention sharing the secrets of survival, sustainability, and happiness.

My ultimate quest is to protect our oceans. Reefs are the rainforests of the sea and provide most of the world's oxygen, and I've witnessed firsthand the detrimental effects from toxic sunscreens, plastic pollution, and climate change. My film on reef protection helped get toxic sunscreens banned in Hawaii, and I'm not stopping there. From Trash Island in the Maldives to the beautiful cenotes in Mexico, water is under threat by the people who need it most—us.

I hope my life will amaze you and inspire you to go on your own adventures and find ways you can help our Earth stay green and blue. So grab your passport and travel around the world with me! (Pink bikinis optional.)

To watch any of my films, visit www.alisonsadventures.com.

CHAPTER ONE

WHEN LIFE HANDS YOU COCONUTS...

HAWAII

I grew up as a world traveler, but I did have a place to call home—Hawaii.

But my story doesn't begin on the Big Island—it begins in Colorado, on the floor of a log cabin high in the Rocky Mountains where I was born during a snowstorm. My mom and papa had spent some time rebuilding an old, tiny miner's cabin in the Rockies. But once I came along and after many years of extreme mountaineering, they were craving warmer climates, sick of frozen pipes and shoveling snow.

They quickly decided on their next adventure, accepting a photo journalism assignment from *Mountain Bike* magazine to take some of the first mountain bikes in the world and the first little Burley cart—the kind that can pull a baby behind a mountain bike—on a three-month camping expedition around the Big Island of Hawaii.

The Big Island has 8 of the 13 ecosystems in the world, and each day was like biking through another country—or planet. There were European-like grasslands, lava fields that felt like the face of Mars, tropical beaches, and dense jungles. These beautiful areas were so welcoming, with Hawaiian uncles and aunties and families that would let us camp in their yards and give us fresh fruit.

One day, in the midst of a near meltdown by toddler me, my parents noticed a narrow lava dirt road in South Kona. They carefully bumped down it a couple of miles, hoping to find a place to camp for the night. When they emerged off the path and onto the ocean, even I forgot my fussiness and took in the sight with wide eyes.

There was a beautiful bay of soft gray sand sprinkled with green crystals that sparkled against the teal blue sea. Swaying palm trees jutted straight up against dark lava cliffs. Spinner dolphins leapt out of the sea, and green sea turtles played in the waves. A few remaining Hawaiian fishing canoes lined the shore. It was one of the last true Hawaiian fishing villages.

They immediately fell in love with it. And I think I did, too.

One night turned into a week. We were camping on a little section of beach in front of a very thick jungle of thorn-ridden kiawe trees when they saw that the property was for sale. Interestingly, the land had never been sold in the history of Hawaii—it still had Queen Liliuokalani's signature on the handwritten title.

The bay used to be a vibrant port city, with a courthouse, a post office, the last Hawaiian-speaking school, and even a church. It was the largest steamship pier in the islands, and legend has it that the queen considered our village a favorite because it was home to so many of her beloved Hawaiian people.

My parents met with the land owner, a Hawaiian elder, and had a *Lion King* moment: suddenly two whales breached in front of the sunset, and the owner said, "This will be yours and your family's." And then it was.

Thereafter, my wild Bohemian papa—who had no architectural schooling—set to work clearing the land manually, with me as a baby on one hip and a machete in his other hand! They respected nature, always doing ceremonies and completing certain rituals, making sure that they weren't disturbing any sacred sites.

queen Liliuokalani

Up until the 1890s, the kingdom of Hawaii remained an independent country. The last to rule this kingdom was Queen Liliuokalani, born Lydia Kamakaeha (1839–1917). She ascended the throne in 1891, the first and only Hawaiian queen to reign.

But she ruled during challenging times under a new Hawaiian constitution that greatly reduced the strength of the monarchy. She fought to restore these powers only to face a U.S. military-backed invasion. To avoid bloodshed, she abdicated the throne and was arrested. A gifted composer and writer, she wrote songs during her imprisonment, including "Aloha oe," and the book *Hawaii's Story by Hawaii's Queen* (1898).

the world is my classroom, and the ocean is my playground.

Right at the end of our beach, there's what's called an "aumakua": a huge carved lava rock shark god that only has its head above the sand, but it has a full shark body and is supposed to protect the bay from sharks. There's never been shark attacks or shark sightings that I know of in that bay. However, one time someone stole it, and as legend goes, you're never supposed to do that with a lava artifact—ever. They had so much death and destruction in their family that they returned it and put it back in the sand!

aumakua

Before Christianity came to Hawaii in 1820, locals worshipped an intricate network of gods and demi-gods based around nature. They also called on aumakua ("spirit guides") for comfort and protection. Aumakua could appear in the form of animals such as owls, lizards, sea turtles, and hawks, and they often used supernatural powers to intercede in human affairs. Many Hawaiians believe aumakua still watch out for them to this day.

We always wanted to give back to the community we were now a part of. My papa provided water for the entire area by raising a grant to get a water line. We also helped with solar power and coral reef preservation, and by creating a nonprofit dedicated to helping preserve Hawaiian culture.

kiawe trees

Believe it or not, every single kiawe tree growing on the Hawaiian Islands today can be traced back to a single sapling planted in a Honolulu churchyard in 1828. Despite the tree's foreign origins, locals quickly realized its wood was the perfect fuel for the imu, a traditional underground oven. In fact, just the smell of burning kiawe wood can make local stomachs rumble for ono ("delicious") food.

I remember my papa sketching out his vision for our house on a napkin—a Robinson Crusoe, Tarzan-esque masterpiece. He drew inspiration from the Amazonian jungle thatched lodges and Indonesian temples. He borrowed a tool belt, harvested bamboo and other sustainable local materials from neighboring farms, collected more than 2,000 palm fronds to be woven for our roofing, and used his climbing ropes from our Himalayan adventures to hang off tall trees and hand build scaffolding to secure the roof.

He did it all with no initial electricity or hand tools. Truly unbelievable!

Over my lifetime, building by building, we created a dream oceanfront retreat in Hawaii that's almost 100 percent sustainable. We call it Hale Kai, which means Ocean House. Our refuge had some of the first solar power in Hawaii, and we can now run lights, refrigerators, and all the comforts of home yet still live with nature and the sun and the ocean.

And, of course, we learned to eat off the land. Based on local organic food, we created a whole food system with recipes for avocado chocolate pies or coconut milk fresh off the coconut trees we planted. Our gardens have mangos, papayas, pineapples, and citrus, as well as tropical flowers that spread a tantalizing aroma of aloha.

kapu & the city of refuge

Kapu embodied an ancient system of laws governing the Hawaiian Islands until 1819. They affected every aspect of life, including religion, politics, and gender roles. Kapu-breakers faced death. That is, unless they could escape to Puʻuhonua o Hōnaunau, the city of refuge. There, they found protection and even forgiveness. What types of things did kapu forbid? Men and women were not allowed to eat together. Women couldn't eat pork, bananas, taro, coconuts, and large or red-colored fish, either. The result? Many Hawaiian women subsisted on seaweeds. While kapu still exist in Hawaii, today they apply to things like trespassing. Fortunately, the punishment is no longer death.

Hale Kai is also where hula dancing and surfing became passions for me. My hula halau (hula group) won statewide competitions when I was only seven. And when most kids were shopping for school clothes and attending school dances, I was learning flower lei making, weaving coconut hats, making grass skirts, and carving coconut bras.

My whole life has been spent immersed in other places and cultures, but the Big Island, Hale Kai, the waves, and the reef—it's the place I call home. It's where my roots are, a familiar place that speaks to my heart and helped make me who I am.

CHAPTER TWO

SCHOOL OF LIFE

NEPAL

One of my greatest dreams as a kid was—and I know this may sound crazy—going to school. Really! I wanted to have textbooks and homework and to sit in a classroom and have friends. I was homeschooled by my parents, and they were great. But I was desperately missing being with people my own age. So when we journeyed to Nepal, I had no idea that my dream was about to come true!

After days of trekking at extreme altitudes alongside massive yaks and crossing rickety rope bridges straight out of an Indiana Jones movie, we made it to Namche Bazaar, a very famous point on the route to Mount Everest—the highest mountain in the world. There's a tea house there called Panorama Tea House, and we pitched our tent nearby, making ourselves as comfortable as we could in the freezing cold and snow.

I'd wake up every morning to my mom doing yoga in the tent and my dad wrestling with his camera and flossing his teeth. To most seven-year-olds, this would have seemed pretty eccentric and wild, but to me, this was normal life.

It wasn't long after we made camp that a terrible blizzard swept through the region, and we decided to wait until the storm subsided before climbing higher. Huddled in our tent in the raging wind, all I could dream about was a far-off reality like school or, better yet, friends.

Wanting an escape from our tent, we made a run through the swirling snow for some hot tea inside the tea house. I remember how the shadows from the yak dung fire danced on the walls as we entered, making it seem a bit mysterious and exciting. But the *most* exciting part for me was when a girl my age brought tea to our table. Her name was Rita, and while we didn't speak the same language, we became instant friends. I was so completely ecstatic to meet someone my age that I volunteered to help serve tea, too.

While waiting out the storm, we drank yak butter tea, which is better than it sounds, and another kind of milk tea. We cooked over yak dung fires, camped out in the cold, and boiled water for our showers, but I was in heaven with my new friend. I didn't think it could get any better until I realized—through our unique communication of gestures and bits of English words Rita had picked up from travelers—that I could go to school with Rita. School. A real school. I was beyond excited!!

Now, school in Namche is very different from the way I had imagined it.

For instance, I didn't expect Rita to shake my tent at 4:00 a.m. Kids didn't go to school that early! But I was undaunted. I hopped out of my sleeping bag, only to be nearly driven back in by the bone-chilling cold. I put on every single piece of clothing I owned, clicked on my headlamp, and followed the dim silhouette of Rita up the mountain.

Before we went too far, Rita gave me some ropes to tie around my shoes to keep me from slipping, kind of like chains on snow tires, and we set off. After walking for what seemed like forever, we suddenly stopped. My fingers and toes were so cold, I thought they would fall off. *If I stop, I'll freeze!* I thought to myself.

Just then, a few other kids joined us for the trek to school. But before we set off again, they took some twigs from their backpacks and made a small fire. It was a lifesaver. The warmth crept back into my fingers and toes, and energized me enough to keep going. After that, we stopped every few hundred yards to make a small fire to warm ourselves enough to continue on.

yak butter tea

Believe it or not, yak butter tea (po cha) is the original "bulletproof coffee," predating today's popular paleo drink by centuries. The high-calorie beverage—made with black tea, salt, yak milk, and, yes, you guessed it, yak butter—originated around the 10th century. Po cha has a thick consistency like soup and combats the frigid temperatures and high elevations of the Nepalese Himalayas.

On May 29, 1953, New Zealander Edmund Hillary (1919–2008) and Nepalese Sherpa Tenzing Norgay (1914–1986) first summitted Mount Everest. The highest point on Earth, they climbed a whopping 29,028 feet above sea level. Hillary went on to climb 10 other Himalayan peaks, reach the South Pole overland (1958), and even search for the abominable snowman (1960).

His adventurous spirit was matched by his generosity. He established the Himalayan Trust, benefiting an estimated 100,000 Nepalese people through the creation of schools, hospitals, medical clinics, and more. In recognition of his philanthropy, he received honorary citizenship to Nepal in 2003.

sir edmund percival hillary

As we went, the little girls and boys that lived in the villages along the way started to come out. By the time we got to the top of the pass, we had quite the crew. It was beautiful up there, with the prayer flags whipping in the (literally) freezing wind. I remember taking a moment to look around. As the sun rose, I felt dwarfed by the majestic mountains surrounding me. We were at 17,000 feet. The beauty was breathtaking, even in the icy breeze.

I had noticed as we walked that each of the kids had huge plastic water jugs that they carried on their backs and I wondered, *Why are they carrying water jugs? Do they need that much water?* Then I realized that they were cut in half. Rita handed one half of hers to me, and before I could even ask her what it was for, she jumped on it and was off, speeding down the mountain at top speed, calling my name to follow her. It was a sled! Maybe not the most normal school transportation, but it looked like fun and was definitely faster than walking.

traditional white sash (khata or khatag)

Traditional white sashes, or khata, symbolize the compassion and purity of the giver. Bestowed to mark major life events (e.g., births, weddings, graduations, funerals), they also show respect and commemorate the arrival or departure of an honored guest. Each khata features the Ashtamangala—eight signs thought to bring good fortune to the receiver.

coat of many colors

We worked with Patagonia on a program where they would make jackets out of the leftover scrap materials from other jackets (hence all the colors), and we would bring them to kids in need all over the world. Here we gifted jackets to the kids in this mountain community.

first lady of everest

On May 16, 1975, Junko Tabei became the first woman to summit Mount Everest. The Japanese mountaineer, who was 35 at the time, led a team of 15 women and 6 Sherpa porters, following the track forged by Sir Edmund Hillary. The party survived being buried by an avalanche en route. In 1992, Tabei became the first woman to scale the tallest mountains on all seven continents.

I jumped on my "sled" and took off after Rita at breakneck speed. I wasn't sure whether to keep my eyes open or closed—the wind made it hard to do either. But it was an exhilarating ride bumping down the hill, eventually coming to a stop just outside of a small building. It was here, at the base of Mount Everest, that Sir Edmund Hillary's Himalayan Trust built a school. Rita's school.

The building itself was a very old, very small, one-level structure with little wooden doors. Maybe it just looked really small because Mount Everest loomed above us, but no matter the size, I wasn't going to miss my first day of school. I scrambled in the door the other students had gone in, too excited for words.

Inside there was an old chalkboard and desks. As I stood there, a little girl came running at me with outstretched arms, and at the last second, instead of welcoming me with a hug, she put a silky white scarf around my neck. It turns out this was actually a traditional white sash (khata or khatag), like the kind the Dalai Lama bestows.

I sat in on the English class, which had 20 to 30 kids, and I remember the teacher was incredibly nervous to teach English in front of me. They would do fun chants to learn and memorize. It was funny because I was mystified by school and they were mystified by me, a little foreign girl— or visitor, Āgantuka (आगन्तुक)—who wanted to go to school with them.

I couldn't wait for recess. I'd dreamed about all the fun games to play with other school kids. Baseball, soccer, tag, playing on the jungle gym—I would have settled for anything. They handed me a rock. Not exactly what I'd seen in Disney movies on the airplanes between adventures, but I was game for playing whatever this was.

It turned out to be a lot like jacks. They'd throw up a rock and then see how many they could pick up before it landed. I wanted to be part of it, trying so hard to understand and learn their game. And they were eager to teach me.

I wanted to give them something for sharing their school day and their kindness with me. I didn't have much, but they were thrilled by my simple gift of a pen and a notebook.

It meant the world to them.

And having friends and going to school meant the world to me.

His Majesty's Government
Ministry of Home
Department of Immigration
(Related to subrule 2 of rule 3)

TREKKING PERMIT

In accordance with the subrule 2 of rule 3 of the Trekking and Rafting rules, 1985 the Permission is hereby granted for trekking in the area of E.V.E.R.E.S.T. .... of the SOLUKHUMBU District from .... to .... 1992 (....21....days) to

CHAPTER THREE

SEARCH FOR THE YETI

NEPAL

You may have heard tales of a large, ape-like creature covered in fur who drags unsuspecting travelers into the depths of its lair high in the Himalayas—the Yeti!

My papa told me stories of the abominable snow creature when I was young to keep me entertained while hiking 10 miles a day in some of the harshest terrain on Earth. I immediately became obsessed, stopping everyone we met along the way (much to the chagrin of my parents) to ask them if they knew where the "ab-dom-inal" snow monster lived.

At night, we made campfires, and Sherpas and traveling yak herders would emerge out of the shadows, seeking warmth from our fire. With wind-burned cheeks and bright eyes, they loved to regale me with more legends and tales. That's when I learned that there was a Yeti skull in a monastery at the base of Mount Everest, and I knew I had to find it.

So, when we went to Nepal, in my parents' mind this trip was for work, to get photographs for different companies and guide some yoga adventures. But in my mind, I was on a search for the Yeti.

We flew in to the small town of Lukla on a tiny, and I do mean tiny, plane. Still one of the most dangerous airports in the world, at that time it was a dirt runway. Although it is now paved, the 2,000-foot drop-off at the end of the runway is still there, as well as the solid stone wall at the other end. Adding to the danger is the lack of radar and navigation devices, making pilots depend only on what they can see from the cockpit. Not exactly the most comforting thought.

As we flew in, it literally looked like we were going to fly into a mountain. And then right before impact, we touched down on a little dirt patch at 9,383 feet, and that's where my search for the Yeti began.

With the story about a Yeti skull at a monastery nearby playing in my head, I begged my parents to let me go check it out. After a lot of persistent persuasion (and maybe a little whining), they finally agreed.

The only way to get there was on foot through the deep Himalayan snow. As we approached the building, it seemed more appropriate for a castle in ancient Europe than a monastery in the Himalayas. I climbed the stone steps of the ancient building, a huge wooden door looming above me. It was more than a little intimidating.

lukla airport

The flight from Kathmandu, Nepal, to the village of Lukla sounds simple enough—a mere 40-minute flight. But when you add the fact that those 40 minutes pass in a blur of white-knuckling and mountain-dodging, you quickly realize why Lukla has the reputation for being the most dangerous airport in the world. What's more, the tiny runway measures no more than 1,720 feet long. For comparison, New York-JFK's shortest runway measures a whopping 8,400 feet.

DANGEROUS LANDING

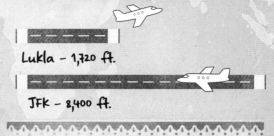

Lukla - 1,720 ft.

JFK - 8,400 ft.

Gathering up my courage, I used all my strength to open the heavy door. Inside, there was only one crooked window high in the corner of the room that shed a beam of light directly onto the altar that held a large golden Buddha. At the base of the Buddha was a row of butter lamps and yak fat candles that sent a spooky, flickering light up onto the Buddha's face, casting strange shadows on it.

The walls held tankas, intricate paintings of religious events done on silk. Many of the painted scenes had skeletons and other scenes of the afterlife. Between the tankas hung ghoulish masks, representing good and evil characters in Buddhist mythology. I could have sworn that some were real human skulls.

On the floor was the only really beautiful thing I saw—a mandala made out of sand. It was about 10 feet across and looked like one of those extremely detailed paint-by-number images. The design was complex, with labyrinths and a lotus at the center of the circle. It was like a small universe. It appeared to be nearly finished—just the very center of the lotus flower was left.

Working on the mandala was one very solemn monk. He was bald and dressed in red robes, and he worked intently, taking no notice of my presence. So I boldly walked over and showed him my sketchbook with a drawing I had made of the Yeti. He still took no notice of me. I showed him again and asked aloud if he would show me the Yeti. Nothing.

Maybe seeing the Yeti skull was not something one just walked up and asked to do. So, I waited.

After what seemed like hours to me, the monk finally stood and approached me, seeming to size me up. His solemn expression still in place, he began to put me through a sequence of tests. I never wanted to pass a test so badly! He had me recite different prayers, help with the mandala, meditate, and light candles. I would have done anything. I was so close! I just had to pass his tests and soon—it was quickly going to be night in one of the coldest places on Earth, and I didn't want to leave without seeing the Yeti skull.

After all his tests, the monk disappeared.

Where could he have gone? Had I earned the right to see the Yeti? I peered around the dark room, my heart sinking and a little sliver of fear creeping in. I was about ready to make a run for the door when he emerged from the shadows carrying a dusty, ornate wooden trunk. It looked like a treasure chest. He stopped, placing the chest in front of me. A shiver of anticipation ran up my spine. My heart was beating fast. I felt just like Indiana Jones.

For the first time since I'd met him, the monk's expression changed. He smiled. Then he opened the trunk and presented to me a brownish scalp with white hair. A Yeti scalp! I almost couldn't breathe. And although I didn't touch it, he let me hold the case that it was in. It was a reverent moment, even for a seven-year-old. I knew that I was seeing something extraordinary, something not many people, especially outsiders, had the opportunity to see.

It was a special moment, made more special by sharing something so sacred. I felt like I'd become part of that cultural family, accepted enough to share some of its deepest secrets. It helped me understand that if you live and align with the culture and respect the people and places around you, what you truly desire will be revealed to you—if you're meant to see it.

yeti

A mysterious bipedal creature covered in dark grayish or reddish-brown fur, the Yeti weighs between 200 and 400 pounds and stands 6 feet tall. Of course, this remains speculation, since most scientists believe it's the stuff of myths. But that hasn't stopped people from claiming to see it. The most recent sighting came in April 2019 when Indian soldiers found its massive footprints, which scientists point out look remarkably like those of a bear.

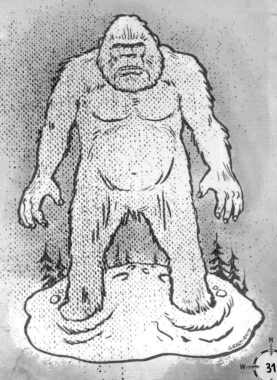

CHAPTER FOUR

FOUNTAIN OF YOUTH

Everyone has heard tales of the fountain of youth—the source of water with magical properties that can keep you young forever. But is it just a myth? Or maybe a hot spring?

Either way, when we visited rural northern India in my childhood, my parents were excited to set off into the remote wilderness. We'd heard about sacred hot springs, though their promises of health and healing sounded a lot to my child brain like the fountain of youth.

We hiked through pine trees and lush foliage over logs through creeks and up rolling green hills and rugged terrain with big boulders. It took a few days, but when we arrived, the sun was starting to set, highlighting the bubbling, natural hot spring nestled against the base of a cliff in a large, grassy valley.

The first thing I did was to go to the shallow end of the hot spring and stick my hand in. The water was crystal clear. It had a perfect, soothing temperature and a strange, almost silky texture. Thick, florescent algae covered the pebble-lined bottom of the spring and glinted magically in the last rays of the sun.

We set up camp close to it, but it wasn't long before a group of men wearing what looked like army uniforms appeared and began building a structure directly over the spring. When they realized we were there, they were surprised by our presence, and their leader came and spoke to us. He told us that the spring was closed, but that perhaps in a few days when the construction was completed we could use it... if we purchased tickets.

They were commercializing the spring!

Disappointed, we went back to camp, preparing to pack up and head out in the morning. The next day, I emerged from the tent to find the beautiful and endless grass fields empty; the log building over and around the spring looked almost complete and screened the water from view. I remember thinking how sad that was.

Mom was meditating on a large rock nearby, oblivious to the explosion of gear all around us; my papa was shooting photos for a lot of different companies, so we had backpacks, climbing gear, shoes, tents, sleeping pads, and sleeping bags everywhere.

Suddenly, a wandering sadhu leaped out of a cave high up on the cliff above us and pranced down the steep slope, boulder to boulder, like a mountain goat. And with a huge final and graceful leap, he landed at our campsite. He was dressed in nothing more than a loin cloth, but he carried an enormous sword.

We had learned that it wasn't unusual for a sadhu to carry a weapon. They often carried swords and other arms as symbols of their identity. This sadhu's sword was immaculate—it didn't seem to have been used, which made me feel a little better. But I was still wary.

what is a sadhu?

For more than 2,000 years, sadhus have wandered the streets of India begging for alms in exchange for blessings and prayers. Considered the holiest men in India, an estimated four to five million exist today. They belong to one of several schools of Hinduism. Draped in saffron robes or wearing a loincloth, many keep their hair in long dreadlocks or sport unkempt beards. Faces marked with sacred ash, their eyes reveal an objective detachment from the world.

Although female sadhus prove rarer, they are known as sadvin and have recently started forming all-female groups. Whether male or female, sadhus lead an ascetic existence. This means cutting all ties with family and friends and rejecting their former lives, careers, and worldly possessions.

northern india's unbelievable climate

When you think about India's climate, what do you picture? Perhaps the lush, palm-filled jungles described in Rudyard Kipling's *The Jungle Book*? In reality, India enjoys an extraordinary variety of climatic regions. These range from tropical areas in the south (most often portrayed in movies and books) to alpine regions in the Himalayan north. Here, you'll find gorgeous mountain forests filled with pine, cedar, spruce, and fir trees.

He was very interested in our huge pile of gear. He sniffed our solar cooker, shook a canteen, clicked a headlamp on and off, and then inquisitively studied the wheels on one of our roller duffels for a moment and then gave each wheel a spin in turn before spinning them all, clearly delighted. Then he suddenly shot to his feet, jumping onto the rock where my mom was meditating, and positioned himself cross-legged next to her. He closed his eyes and began to meditate, too.

With his photographer's instincts, my papa thought it would be a great idea to have me sitting with them and take some pictures. I didn't want to sit for pictures. I wanted a chance to hold that big sword! But if I learned nothing else traveling with my parents, I'd learned that we did whatever it took to get the shot, so I climbed up and joined them. Neither of them moved.

I closed my eyes, pretending to meditate, and nearly jumped out of my skin when I felt a pinch on my cheek. My eyes flew open to find the sadhu grinning at me. He gently tugged on a strand of my blond hair, and then tugged at a strand of his black hair as if mesmerized by the color difference. I don't know if he'd seen many Caucasian people, let alone a little seven-year-old one with freckles and blond hair.

I tried communicating with my new-found friend, though he didn't speak very much English. I kept trying to ask how old he was. I would write my age in the dirt, show him my age on my fingers. He showed me on his fingers a one then a four and then a five. That made no sense to me. 145? No one was that old, but he nodded, insisting this was his age. Maybe he really was a product of the hot springs— having used the water to keep himself young. Maybe it really did make him magically invincible.

the railroad for billions

India's railway network carries a record 8 billion people every year over 41,861 miles of railway tracks. The densest, longest network in the world, the tracks would circle the Earth nearly 1.5 times if laid out end-to-end.

Whether his real age was 145 or not, he definitely had a connection to the springs and didn't like the construction and commercialization that was happening there, either. He seemed a little fiery and wild—you could see it in his eyes—and he seemed to have deemed himself the protector of this holy spring.

After his visit, as we prepared to break camp and move on, we saw him coming down from his cave on the cliffs again. This time, he pranced from rock to rock but leapt onto the top of the newly built cabin over the spring. Before we knew what was happening, the entire building went up in flames, and he stood there in the middle of it on the roof with the flames licking up all around him. It was terrifying and surreal.

And as suddenly as he was there, he wasn't. He disappeared as the men who built the structure came running to see what was happening.

We never saw him again.

Just before we left, I put a drawing I had made in his cave, hoping that he really was magically invincible and that he would escape unharmed.

I remember after that thinking that when you live in India, you just start to believe in the magic—you believe that anything is possible, even a man living to be 145.

CHAPTER FIVE

COBRA KISS

MOROCCO

I have a confession to make. As a child, I was completely and utterly obsessed with *Aladdin*. The turbans. The markets teeming with people and vendors and all sorts of spices and things to buy. Jasmine and that unforgettable carpet ride. And who could forget Abu? I absolutely loved all of it!

That love has lasted into my adulthood. It wasn't long after I was out of film school that I traveled with my family to Morocco. We planned to start in Marrakech and then go on a surf safari (I like to call it a surf-ari) down the Moroccan coastline. Known for uncrowded beaches and some of the best surfing off the coast of Africa, the chance to experience this wild, amazing landscape firsthand was an opportunity I couldn't pass up.

Our guide first took us to a market in Marrakech—I was enchanted! It looked like it was straight out of *Aladdin*, with men playing the pungi flute, monkeys jumping around, and snake charmers. It smelled of oranges, with so many carts selling the fruit for fresh-squeezed juice.

The paths through the market reminded me of tunnels—tight and winding but filled with the most extravagant, magical-looking shops. I could almost believe that a flying carpet would swoop by! The shops were filled with lots of different items, from decorative lighting to (what else!) rugs. They sold lamps that looked just like the genie's lamp in my favorite movie.

Other parts of the market were out in the open, and there was a man there surrounded by iguanas and reptiles of all sorts, as well as herbs and spices. My papa told us that he was a faith healer. In many cultures, instead of going to a doctor for a diagnosis, people go to a healer who prescribes cures or bestows healings.

A little bit of a crowd had drawn, and he was talking very fast in his own language and moving his arms. I wasn't sure what he was talking about, but then he singled me out. His motions became wilder and more frenetic. He was concerned for me, he said. He told me that I was in danger of having a serious surfing accident... if I didn't kiss a live cobra snake.

Now, there was no way he could have known I was a surfer. Though I usually have my pink surfboard with me, I wasn't walking around with it in the Marrakech market that day. And we were more than 100 miles from the ocean. So this statement struck me as a little weird.

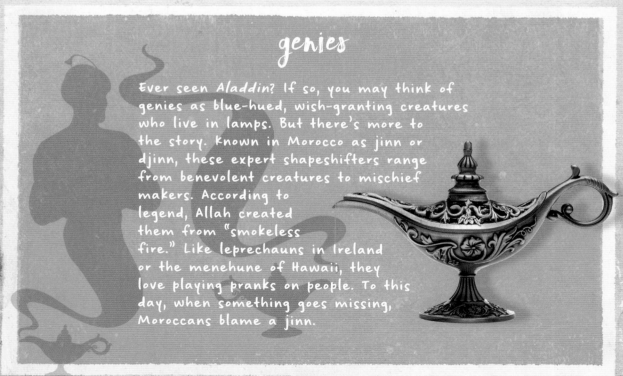

genies

Ever seen Aladdin? If so, you may think of genies as blue-hued, wish-granting creatures who live in lamps. But there's more to the story. Known in Morocco as jinn or djinn, these expert shapeshifters range from benevolent creatures to mischief makers. According to legend, Allah created them from "smokeless fire." Like leprechauns in Ireland or the menehune of Hawaii, they love playing pranks on people. To this day, when something goes missing, Moroccans blame a jinn.

He then told me to look for rainbows, saying, "they will guide your journey," which I thought was ironic because Hawaiians believe similarly that rainbows are signs and omens.

When he told me that I had to kiss a snake to avoid this calamity, my first thought was, *Oh, that sounds like a bit of a gamble. I can either die in the ocean from a surfing accident or I could die kissing the snake right now.* But my parents raised me with a sense to believe in the superstition and supernatural to a point—you don't want to do anything too crazy. Kissing a live cobra sounded a little crazy.

But he was very adamant about it. So I asked him where we would find a cobra, and before I knew it, he whipped out this large cobra snake and a viper snake. He told me I might as well kiss both just to be safe. Really?!

I remember the sound of tribal music playing on flutes and drums as I stood there looking at the snakes, their heads darting here and there. The healer grabbed the neck of one and held it out to me. The snake's tongue was flicking in and out, and all I could think was, *Oh, this is strange.* But I didn't really feel scared. I was wrapped up in the magic of the moment. So I did it. I kissed the cobra snake and the viper snake.

After that, we went on our merry way. A few days later, we were traveling down the Moroccan coastline, going by car and by camel, of course, with my pink surfboard made out of coffee cups and my camel named Boom Boom.

We stopped at Anchor Point, which is a pretty famous spot now. At that time, it wasn't as discovered, so it was still pretty desolate. The waves were massive, and it was incredibly windy. It's very desert-like along the coastline—a harsh landscape with very cold water. It's not how you might imagine Africa to be.

Although the locals told me that not a lot of women surfed there, I wasn't worried. From what I could see, the waves didn't seem as large as what I was used to in Hawaii. And I'd come all this way to surf Morocco, so I jumped off a rock, paddled out, and within seconds, the current swept me really far down the coast. I thought to myself, *Maybe this isn't the best idea*. But I was determined.

When I finally paddled out there against the current, the waves were so pretty and huge and, honestly, kind of scary. I went to take off—but what I didn't realize is that if you fall or anything happens on the takeoff, you go straight into this rock called Anchor Point.

Now, when I looked at it from the shore, it didn't give me a sense of imminent doom. But I soon discovered that it definitely should have.

Of course, I fell on the takeoff and was sucked straight into the rock then straight to the bottom, the water throwing me around like a ragdoll. I don't know how long I was down there being tossed around by the waves, but it felt like an eternity. I remember thinking, *This is the end. I'm going to die.*

pirate haven

The Moroccan town of Essaouira lies 2 ½ hours away from Marrakech and was once an important ancient trading seaport where pirates were said to take refuge. Sugars and spices were carted into the city's stone fort, protected behind the walled city complete with cannons on the ramparts. Medieval maps show the city was called Mogador, which originated from the Berber word for "safe anchorage." Today, it's a fishing village where tourists come to enjoy the pristine beaches and epic wind surfing.

I was completely disoriented and had no idea which way was up. I was worrying that I was going to black out from a lack of oxygen when suddenly I saw a faint rainbow. *Swim toward the rainbow*, I thought. As I was struggling toward it, I hit something and heard an alarmingly loud crack. Was that my neck? Or my back? It's nearly impossible to tell when you're underwater and everything is so disorienting.

It all happened quickly, but I just kept remembering the healer's words and following the rainbow. Before I knew it, I popped up out of the water.

At that moment, I realized I had quite the audience on the shore that had come to see what had happened. I learned later that they all thought I was done for. They were standing around trying to figure out how to find my body and bring me in.

Somehow, I just floated in to the beach. As the water got shallower, I put my feet on the sand. When I walked out of the water, everybody was in shock. One guy exclaimed, "I don't know how you just survived that!"

And I didn't either.

Then I looked at my board. The fin had cracked out—so that was the mysterious crack I had heard underwater—but other than that, I didn't have a single scratch, bruise, or break.

I sat down where I was, looked up at the camel and the camel driver, looked out at the ocean and the palm trees, and, incredibly, saw another rainbow. This one seemed to start in the ocean and stretch back over the land toward Marrakech.

Was that faith healer right? Or did I just get lucky? If I hadn't kissed that snake—or both of them—would I be dead on the bottom of the Moroccan ocean? You really can't help but wonder.

It always makes me think that if you just believe or at least trust in the unknown, you can have some pretty incredible experiences. It wasn't a magic carpet ride, but it was my own bit of Moroccan magic.

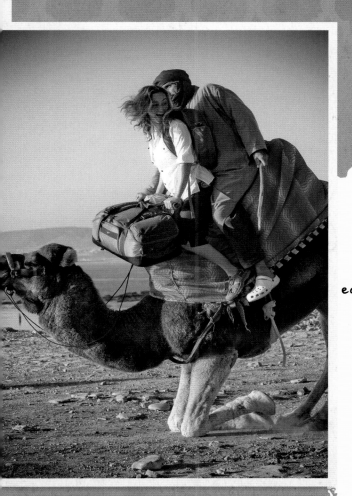

camels

Camels are perfectly suited for arid deserts. They can drink up to 40 gallons of water at a time and store more than 80 pounds of fat in their humps. This allows them to go for weeks or even months without eating. They have three sets of eyelids and two rows of eyelashes to protect against sand and can even shut their nostrils during sandstorms. Domesticated 4,000 years ago by humans, they remain an important form of transportation in Morocco.

CHAPTER SIX

The Mystery at
BLUE DUCK
STATION

NEW ZEALAND

There is still a place on Earth where the land and waters are pristine, where the beauty of nature is breathtaking. From beautiful coasts with great surfing to misty mountains with legendary views, New Zealand is truly stunning.

After taking some time to surf in this amazing area, you can imagine that I became curious about what the land was like here, too. I'd heard about the mountains and the farms and the sheep, and this surfer girl was ready to see what New Zealand farming was all about.

With my pink surfboard under my arm, I headed for Blue Duck Station, a conservation farm that was home to lots of endangered wildlife and animals native to New Zealand. It's called Blue Duck Station because part of its mission is to help raise and protect blue ducks, which is an indicator species for New Zealand. That means that if the blue duck disappears, then the health of the environment is in serious trouble.

The most landlocked farm on the North Island of New Zealand, Blue Duck was owned and operated by Dan Steele, who kindly allowed me to drop in and get a taste of farm life. He quickly introduced me to his right-hand man, Cowboy Chad, who was glad to have an extra hand himself. It seemed there was a mystery afoot at the farm—cows and sheep had been mysteriously disappearing from their pastures. Not only did he need help finding them and getting them back where they belonged, but also he needed to find out why they were disappearing, and fast.

As it happened, the Minister of Conservation was due to pay a visit to the farm in the next few days. For a visit like this, everything needed to be perfect—this was more like an evaluation of how well the farm was doing its job in keeping endangered animals and their environment safe and in great shape. Having animals escaping wouldn't make a great impression at all. And a bad impression could mean no government funds, which would put the future of the entire farm at stake!

Not wanting to fail in our mission to solve the mystery and save the farm, we got to work right away. Dressed in cowboy boots and a hat, Chad strapped a leather belt around his waist, tucking his trusty walkie-talkie in the holster, and we were off. With the farm dogs leading the way, we headed out to check on the most recent mystery—a missing herd of cows.

As we trudged up muddy hills past fences and pastures and into more remote territory, I couldn't help but feel like I was in a Western. All I was missing was a cowboy hat. And a horse. But that would come soon enough.

Used to catching waves, I definitely wasn't used to catching sheep. Or cows. But I was about to get seriously outside of my comfort zone, which, according to Cowboy Chad, is a good thing. He told me we were going to muster these cows once we found them.

Muster? This was apparently New Zealand for round up.

We walked for hours up a steep mountainside. Something seemed familiar. When I remarked on it to Chad, he told me that this was the area where they'd filmed *The Lord of the Rings* movies. That was it! Being in it was definitely surreal. I would have loved more time to just take it all in, but I knew I had to focus on the important task at hand.

I asked Chad if there was a way to find the cows we were looking for. He said we simply had to moo like a cow. And then he demonstrated, letting out a deep, long moooooo. Nothing. Not a single cow in sight.

lord of the rings filming

From 2001 to 2003, the otherworldly landscapes of New Zealand took center stage in the *Lord of the Rings* trilogy as the fabled haunts of Middle Earth. The jagged, snowy peaks of Queenstown became the Pillars of Argonath and the Eregion Hills. The rolling emerald hills of Matamata in the North Island transformed into Hobbiton, a peaceful town in the Shire, and the volcanic region of Mount Ruapehu became fiery Mount Doom, where Sauron forged the Ring. All told, more than 150 locations in New Zealand can be seen in the *Lord of the Rings* trilogy. Today, you can still visit many of these spots on a guided tour of the countryside.

Hmm. I wasn't sure if he'd been teasing or not, but we'd been walking for quite a while. It took my secret stash of dark chocolate and a little more mud in our shoes to get us to the top of the mountain before trying the call again. This time I joined in, Chad giving me tips on the finer points of mooing, when out of the trees a cow emerged. It actually worked!

I was now obsessed with mooing, and as I kept calling out to them, more cows showed up until we were completely surrounded. It was a little intimidating. The cows were large, and they'd made a ring around us. I wasn't quite sure what we were going to do now that we'd found them, but we were clearly outnumbered. And the cows knew it.

Just as they started to move in, I jumped for the closest tree, escaping the thundering stampede below me. From the safety of my perch, I watched with relief as Chad took control of the situation using whistles and commands for the dogs. They jumped into action, herding the cows and neatly helping us steer this large group down the mountainside. Chad made sure they stampeded through the right gate and back into their pasture with its newly mended fence. One mission accomplished!

Exhausted and hungry, we were about to head back for some much-needed food, but before we could, Chad's walkie-talkie crackled to life. He whipped our lifeline to the farm from its holster, only to hear boss Dan telling us that we had a new problem. Some of their horses had gotten out of their holding paddock and were running wild. How had they gotten out? No one was sure, but it was up to me and Chad to muster them back into their paddock.

With a storm brewing overhead, we hurried back to saddle up our horses, because we'd have no chance of catching them on foot. With our herding dogs close by and the sky pouring buckets of rain, we rode out into the forest. We were soaked in no time. The rain in our eyes and the constant spray of mud from our galloping horses didn't deter us from riding hard to catch up to the escaped horses. Now I was in that Western—Yippee-ki-yay!

And then in a movie-worthy moment, the herd of lost horses materialized out of the mist and rain. The wind whipped their drenched manes and tails as they raced toward us at breakneck speed. As we reached them, Chad called the dogs into action and we all worked together to surround them on all sides, effectively stopping their stampede and gaining a tenuous hold on them as a group.

Still wild and looking for any way out of our circle, the horses pranced and panted, hooves stomping hard as we herded them along, but suddenly there was a creek none of us had expected. And, as though we'd rehearsed it, the dogs, the horses, and Chad and I leapt as one to the opposite bank, where we funneled the horses into the newly repaired paddock where they belonged. Another mission under our belts, we were still no closer to figuring out why the animals kept escaping. Why were the fences being damaged? How were we going to solve that mystery?

We didn't have time to think about it just then. The storm was relentless, and we were still a distance from the farm. Chad repeatedly tried to radio Dan, but there was no signal. Resigning ourselves to the fact that we couldn't call for help, we took shelter inside the only structure nearby—a creepy-looking cabin.

Known locally as The Depot, our shelter had been the tiny shack that once housed important things like whiskey, mail, and even ammunition. Now there were only bits of broken glass from old bottles, rusted horseshoes, and a large sign clearly stating "Explosives." The combination of the weather, our rundown cabin, and my own hunger left me feeling uneasy.

blue duck station

Located on the banks of the Whanganui and Retaruke Rivers, Blue Duck Station is a haven for endangered wildlife and nature enthusiasts. The station aims to preserve the history of the surrounding area, educate its visitors, and aid in conservation efforts of animals like the blue duck and kiwi birds, as well as wetas (giant flightless crickets), bats, and fish native to New Zealand. If you're ever in the area, give tramping a go—"tramping" is the New Zealand term for backpacking!

As the storm raged outside, we made ourselves as comfortable as we could. Using a little ingenuity and water from Chad's canteen, we enjoyed some hot tea in our tight quarters. Just as we began to settle in, Chad's walkie-talkie let out an ear-piercing screech, scaring us both to death. It was Dan! But he wasn't coming to our rescue—he had solved the mystery of the animals on the loose! It seemed that a band of wild sheep was breaking fences and wreaking havoc on the farm. The only way to stop them was to catch the head sheep.

It was last seen on the mountain above our creepy cabin.

The storm outside was dying down, and the evening darkness had started to fall. It didn't make much sense to try going back to the farm when we were so close to the wild sheep. There wasn't much time before the Minister was due to visit. We had to catch that head sheep quickly and make sure the farm was in perfect condition.

We didn't have anywhere to sleep—there wasn't room in the cabin. The storm had gone and the stars had come out, so we hunkered down outside in the cold. We covered ourselves in horse blankets and built a small fire to try to stay warm. We would work on catching the wild sheep in the morning. With the flames of our fire casting spooky shadows everywhere, the strange sounds of the New Zealand forest around us, and the many myths and mysteries of this area bouncing around my head, it was nearly impossible to sleep.

But I must have slept at least a little, because Chad woke me before daybreak. Overnight, the fog had set in thick and dark, so that it was difficult to see even with our headlamps. We mounted our horses and set out in the murky mist. A shiver ran down my spine, and I struggled to keep Chad and the dogs in sight.

Thankfully, daylight soon lit the sky. We put away our headlamps, and Chad distracted me from the gloomy, dark corners of the forest by telling me about the kiwi bird. Since the birds are nocturnal, you could hear them calling at night. Just when I was feeling at ease thinking about little kiwi birds in the forest, the terrain changed dramatically, becoming so steep that our horses began to slip and slide.

Chad leapt off of his saddle and called back to me that we would have to continue on foot. We tied the horses securely to a tree and set off, Chad assuring me that they would be safe until we returned.

The air was cold and damp, chilling us to the bone, but we forged ahead, determined to complete our mission. Suddenly, Chad stopped—he'd found fresh tracks! Showing me the messy swirls of mud and hoof tracks, we knew we were close.

It was at this point that Chad took a moment to educate me on the finer points of catching wild sheep. He said that they should be flipped onto their backs, because they're docile in that position. I wasn't quite sure how you did that, but I'm sure Chad did, and that's what mattered.

Also, if something were to come out and charge at me, he said I should just try to get out of the way, because these sheep were huge and capable of mowing down anything in their path. This tip was more alarming, and it occurred to me that this would have been useful information to have had before we were so close to attempting to catch one! Why was he just now sharing this with me? And what else did I need to know?

As I posed this all-important question, Chad began to answer but was cut short as he disappeared from my view momentarily. He came back into sight, rolling down the hill as the herd of wild sheep in question began stampeding down the hill over us.

"Flip the sheep over!" Chad managed to yell as he tumbled head over heels. What? Was he crazy? These weren't just your average, run-of-the-mill sheep. These sheep were massive! Imagine a cow-sized, matted ball of wet, heavy wool on four legs. Then imagine an entire herd of them running toward you—for a brief moment I was too terrified to move.

Remembering Chad's instructions to get out of the way, I dove toward the only tree near me, only to be joined by the largest of the flock, who was attempting to charge me. Her desire to cause mischief finally caught up with her as she became hopelessly entangled in the small tree, too. This was the massive marauding head sheep we had been searching for!

Unhurt, Chad made his way back up to where the enormous sheep and I were eyeballing each other skeptically. We wrenched her out of the tree and flipped her over. Chad was right—she was much more docile this way. But how were we going to haul her down the steep, muddy mountainside? She was bigger than both of us combined.

Chad grabbed the head, avoiding her large teeth, and I managed to hold the smelly, dense wool on her back side. We started our slow descent with our captive in tow. She was dragging us more than we were carrying her. It was slow going, and she kept trying to bolt, forcing us to stop frequently and calm her down. We got some distance down the hill when she bolted again. I lunged and grabbed at her, desperately trying to keep her from escaping, when she pulled the both of us into a hole.

Fortunately for me, I ended up on top. But she squirmed and bleated, making it nearly impossible for me to climb out. Chad grabbed my arm and managed to haul me out. We clung to the sheep while Chad grabbed his trusty walkie-talkie and radioed Dan for some back up. We spent what felt like an eternity on the edge of that hole, assessing our wounds and catching our breath until finally Dan appeared out of the thicket. With renewed strength, we were able to move our new wooly friend to a well-fenced pasture. The mystery was solved, and this rogue sheep would no longer cause trouble for Blue Duck Station.

Exhausted, we longed for a hearty, hot meal and a much-needed rest. We'd been up and down mountains, through rain and mud, and slept under the stars. We'd corralled cows, horses, and sheep. We ensured that the farm would be safe. And we'd done it all before the Minister arrived. We couldn't have been more pleased with ourselves.

Then Chad's walkie-talkie erupted with static and chatter. Dan had one more critical mission for us: locate a blue duck to take the Minister to see when she arrived.

What? How do you find one? And if you do, how do you get it to stay?

But there was no time for questions. Chad and I were off again, this time on kayaks. As we paddled down the narrow Whanganui River, Chad began to warn me about the massive eels native to these waters. Slowly Chad's voice became harder and harder to hear, and I finally realized why: we were getting dangerously close to a waterfall, and the thundering water became nearly deafening.

We were able to jam our kayaks in the rocks just before we would have been sucked right over the falls. We climbed out of our boats and looked over the edge, mesmerized by the beauty and power of the rushing water, when we both saw it—perched on a log in the pond below us was the blue duck we'd been searching for!

blue ducks

Known as the whio by the Maori, the blue duck is a unique species found nowhere else on Earth but New Zealand. They get their name from their plumage, which looks slate gray in the light and allows them to blend into river rocks. To thrive, the whio needs plenty of fast-flowing, clear water and are known as torrent ducks. As a result, about 10 of the 1,400 remaining pairs of blue ducks can be found living along the rivers on Blue Duck Station, where conditions prove ideal.

Excitedly, we noted the location and prayed that the duck wouldn't move. We rushed back to the farm to meet the Minister, who had just arrived. With her and her entire entourage in tow, we headed back out, hoping that our blue duck was still there. If we could show the duck, it would prove that the conservation efforts of the farm were working.

I held my breath as we neared the spot. There wasn't a blue duck there anymore. There were two! The Minister and her group were elated. Chad and I were nearly delirious with joy and exhaustion. We had ensured the future of Blue Duck Station. Mission definitely accomplished!

As I reflected on my time on the farm, I realized that it's not just about me and Chad saving the day. It's about saving the entire ecosystem. It's about all of us working together to protect this beautiful planet that provides us life. It's mind-blowing to me how interconnected everything is in our world. Blue Duck Station is a microcosm of that—if the blue duck goes extinct, an entire country could be in trouble, sending ripple effects around the world.

On a global scale, we depend upon the planet and the animals for our survival, and in turn, we must protect and take care of them. If we upset the balance of the environment, we create a situation where living beings cannot survive. Each species on the planet plays a part in keeping the health of our planet in balance, including us.

We don't always understand how much each one of us can really affect the world around us. Even I couldn't believe that my time lending a hand at Blue Duck could have a greater planetary benefit, but it was the most rewarding feeling to know that it had!

This adventure truly taught me that if we step outside our comfort zone, embrace change, and do something, even a little thing, we can all have a big impact in this world and bring us closer to that all-important balance. Even a surfer girl trying her hand at ranching.

CHAPTER SEVEN

VOLCANO SURF

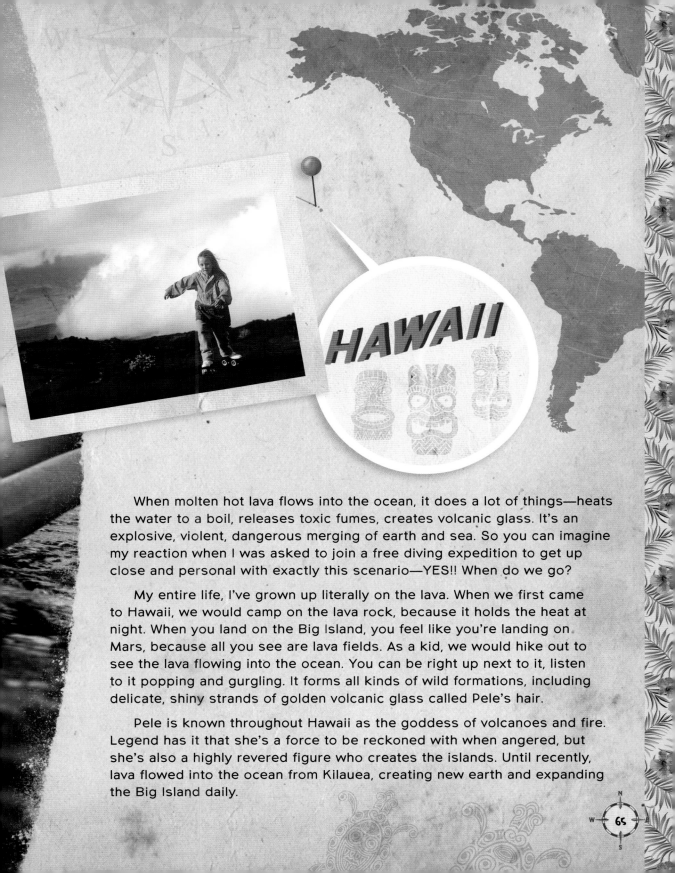

HAWAII

When molten hot lava flows into the ocean, it does a lot of things—heats the water to a boil, releases toxic fumes, creates volcanic glass. It's an explosive, violent, dangerous merging of earth and sea. So you can imagine my reaction when I was asked to join a free diving expedition to get up close and personal with exactly this scenario—YES!! When do we go?

My entire life, I've grown up literally on the lava. When we first came to Hawaii, we would camp on the lava rock, because it holds the heat at night. When you land on the Big Island, you feel like you're landing on Mars, because all you see are lava fields. As a kid, we would hike out to see the lava flowing into the ocean. You can be right up next to it, listen to it popping and gurgling. It forms all kinds of wild formations, including delicate, shiny strands of golden volcanic glass called Pele's hair.

Pele is known throughout Hawaii as the goddess of volcanoes and fire. Legend has it that she's a force to be reckoned with when angered, but she's also a highly revered figure who creates the islands. Until recently, lava flowed into the ocean from Kilauea, creating new earth and expanding the Big Island daily.

Our house is in one of the ancient lava
flows, so it was always something I dreamed about—to be at that
point where the hot lava flows into the ocean, to watch the Earth being born and
really be at one with the elements.

With our plan in place to dive and record what the ecosystem around the heated
water looked like, we went to one of the most revered Hawaiian families to get the proper
blessings and permission. As advised, we brought the appropriate offerings of different
alcohols and salts, sang specific chants, following all the protocols as instructed to be
respectful of Pele.

Our small group traveled for hours on a small boat bouncing through standing waves,
until we reached where the volcano had been erupting and spilling into the ocean. But the
visibility was poor—there was no way to photograph or shoot anything underwater. We
couldn't even see our hands in front of our faces.

I was so disappointed that we couldn't dive! But I had my pink surfboard with me, as
I always do, and I had this urge to paddle out and get closer. I wanted to be one with the
Earth and just give thanks to Pele.

pele, the goddess of fire

The goddess of fire and volcanoes, Pele or Pelehonuamea ("she who shapes the sacred land") remains the most visible of all the ancient Hawaiian deities. According to legend, she lives with her family of fire gods in one of the most volatile volcanoes in the world, at the summit of Kilauea in the Halema'uma'u Crater.

Pele controls the volcano's lava flow and is known for her unpredictable and passionate temper. Yet visitors who stand at the edge of the crater also report feeling deeply moved by the spirit of the goddess. While Pele continues to devour the Big Island with molten lava, according to Hawaiian lore, this volcanic activity has also resulted in 70 new acres of land along the southeastern coast since 1983 alone.

In Hawaiian culture, they say that if Pele doesn't want you there, it'll be known. There are stories of things that have happened where people will be trying to bulldoze land that was sacred to her and suddenly the bulldozers would break or the person would have a stroke or something bad thing would happen. I felt a bit uneasy.

As soon as I jumped off the boat, a double rainbow appeared directly over us. In ancient Hawaiian culture, rainbows represent the way that the gods would come down to the island. I took that as a good sign, and paddled out and watched the rainbow.

heat and haze

Although volcanoes produce life, they are definitely dangerous, especially up close. The temperature of erupting Kilauea lava is more than 2,000°F, and the lava traveling to the sea doesn't get much cooler—that is, until it hits air and the cold sea, which is when the lava cools as fast as hundreds of degrees per second. At the same time, the meeting of molten rock and salty sea creates "laze" or lava haze—a poisonous plume of white smoke that contains volcanic glass shards smaller than grains of sand and hydrochloric acid. The lava haze is hazardous to anyone nearby.

It is also said in Hawaii that Pele will present herself somehow in the lava and the rocks. If you look carefully on the video we recorded, you can see her face in the dripping lava: two glowing eyes and her hair. You can call me crazy, but I felt a connection, as if she was saying, *We're going to need strong females to protect the earth that I'm birthing*, as if giving me a mission and a confirmation to keep doing what I'm doing to help protect the planet and inspire future generations.

An hour later, that entire shelf collapsed, and had I been there, I would have been killed.

pele's hair

Hawaii's volcanoes can put on quite a show. They shoot incandescent lava sprays hundreds of feet into the air or send molten lava flows cascading over sheer cliffs into the steaming ocean below. These incredible displays even result in "Pele's hair," spiderweb-thin strands of volcanic glass resembling coarse, gossamer-colored human hair. Drifts of these interwoven "goddess" locks can measure one to two feet thick, carpeting the ground in Hawaii.

The time I spent out there was exhilarating and a bit terrifying. At one point, I had to dive underwater to avoid a flying lava rock that exploded near me. And another moment, I almost got caught by a wave and smashed into the flow. Overall, I just felt protected. If you think too much about something, you might not do it. In life I take caution, but I also feel when I'm supposed to do something, and this was one of those times I felt like I was supposed to.

Just to look up at waterfalls of hot molten lava pouring down 150-foot cliffs in front of me, listening to the sound of the crackle and the pop and the hiss and the unknown—it was humbling. It was powerful. I was watching the new earth being born. It was truly one of the most profound experiences of my life.

CHAPTER EIGHT

LEGEND OF THE FIRE WALKERS

According to legend, long ago a fisherman had gone out fishing and caught an eel. As he was about to kill the eel to bring it back to his chief, the eel begged for its life, promising to give the fisherman and his people the power to walk on fire and heal with touch.

The fisherman rushed the eel back to the chief, excitedly explaining what had happened. He anxiously awaited the chief's sage advice. The chief decided to spare the eel's life, and ever since then, the people of the island were granted the powers the eel promised.

When I heard that this legend was true, that there was a place on Earth where some of the last fire walkers still practiced the ancient and magical art, I had to go there and see it for myself.

It turns out that the adventure began with the journey, as I rode sketchy busses on winding roads, sailed on pirate ship–like boats, took hand-carved canoes, and, for the finale, tucked into a tiny rowboat during a torrential downpour. But as the tropical storm cleared, a tiny, remote island appeared, and I breathed a sigh of relief.

As I set foot on the safety of the shore, I admired the white sand cove and the numerous palm trees overflowing with coconuts. The entire area was incredibly beautiful except for the coral reef, which looked dead. I only had a moment to wonder about it before I really started to wonder about the lack of people. There didn't seem to be anyone on this island.

I seemed to be completely alone.

Although I felt a bit uneasy, I knew it would be dark soon, and I would need shelter and food. I grabbed a coconut and set up my survival hammock. I would do some exploring in the morning and see if I could find any signs of life. While being alone here made me nervous, the thought of meeting members of the tribe was a bit nerve-wracking, too. I had heard rumors that the people here were cannibals. Not the most reassuring thought as darkness began to set in for the night.

I struggled to sleep, with the moonlight creating spooky shadows through the palm leaves. Every noise from the jungle around me made me snuggle tighter into the security of my hammock. When I woke in the morning, I heard a distant drum beat—a ga-donk ga-donk ga-donk, almost like war drums. I definitely wasn't alone.

Unsure if the primitive sound I was hearing was war drums or something else, I followed it through the jungle, climbing up and over and through trees and vines and vegetation. Soon I arrived in a small, traditional village on a bay and came face-to-face with three very large, very fierce-looking Fijian men with huge mallets raised high above their heads. They seemed unconcerned at my presence, continuing to pound the mallets on massive, hollowed-out logs.

But they weren't declaring war—they were sounding the church bells. The villagers are devoted Christians. The "bells" brought people into the village center, and as we all gathered, they welcomed me, wanting to meet and talk with me. It was here that I met the chief of the village. Maybe he could tell me about fire walking!

He invited me to join them all for a meal of cassava with tapioca, coconut milk, and fish. I waited as long as I could to ask if I could interview him. He agreed, and I introduced the topic of fire walking. I could barely contain my excitement as he began to tell me about it, detailing the long history. But to my great surprise and disappointment, he told me that his tribe hadn't walked on fire for 20 years!

4

I'd come all this way and they didn't walk on fire anymore? Surely if they had the magical ability to do it, they could still perform the ritual? Bravely, I asked if he would be willing to break their 20-year hiatus and show me how they walk on fire. I held my breath during the long moments of silence as he thought it over. The moments seemed endless, and for a while I thought he wasn't going to respond.

But finally he turned to me, a mysterious look in his eyes, and asked me to come with him. He said that we were going to bring kava to the chief. Wait. Wasn't he the chief? But then he told me that in Fiji there were many chiefs. How many, I wasn't sure, and why we were going to bring kava to this chief, I wasn't sure of either, but if it might mean learning more about fire walking, I was in.

Before I knew it, we headed out in the pouring rain to bring kava to another chief and perform an entire kava ceremony. The elders of the village sat in a circle chanting a special call and response phrase in Fijian and clapping along rhythmically. They passed around a coconut-shell cup full of what I learned was ground kava root but looked and tasted like muddy water.

kava ceremonies

Considered by locals to be the "national drink" of Fiji, kava (yaqona in Fijian) represents more than just a muddy-looking, bitter beverage with mild sedative properties. An entire ceremony surrounds its consumption, representing a crucial part of daily life and good etiquette in Fiji. When visiting a new village, you should give a small gift (sevusevu) of kava root to the chief.

During the kava ceremony, participants sit cross-legged on the floor in a circle in front of the chief. He mixes the root, first pounded into a fine powder, with water. This mixture is then strained through a cloth into a bilo (a bowl made from half a coconut shell) and passed from drinker to drinker. Before accepting the bilo, each participant claps once, drinks the contents of the bowl, then claps again and exclaims, "Bula!" When handing back the bowl, the person claps three more times and the group joins in.

This ceremony was held to call in the magical power of the ancestors. I watched and smiled and drank the kava when it came around to me. I left with my tongue numb from the effects of the kava, but potentially one step closer to seeing real fire walking.

After the ceremony, the chief and I boarded a little boat and headed out on the reef. Without much explanation, he handed me a hammer and a nail, and he told me to dive down. What was I supposed to do with these tools underwater? When I asked, he simply said, "We're replanting the reef."

Their reef had been destroyed by climate change, storms, and plastics. So we dove down with pieces of living coral and pounded them into the reef, hoping that they would take root and flourish. I felt honored to be a part of the important task of repairing the environment that supported all life for this tiny island. The chief and I shared a smile as we finished, and a little piece of my world shifted—I felt like I'd started becoming part of this island family.

When I came to this island, I knew that I couldn't just come in as an outsider and expect to immediately see something that's sacred. It was much like my Yeti skull experience—to gain their trust, to be privileged to share in something revered by them, I would have to go through a certain process and, essentially, become accepted within their tribe.

On my road to acceptance, there were more quests to fulfill. For the next one, the chief had me meet him in the village—he wanted to take me and his kids to see the head chief. He said we didn't need to bring kava, but that we did have to bring the Christian minister. I was a little confused. Wasn't kava an essential part of meeting all the chiefs? Why did we need a minister? And just how many chiefs were there?

At first, I thought we were going to another island to a big church, but I couldn't have been more wrong! We set off into the jungle with machetes and flashlights, scrambling over rocks and through jungle-like vegetation with all of the chief's kids in tow—one of them on his hip. We made it around to the other side of the island to the mouth of a very dark cave.

We stopped at the opening, and the minister said a blessing in Fijian. My excitement level was building. What could be in this cave? A sacred statue? A priceless artifact? It had to be something really important. Then the chief told us, "I need you all to turn your headlamps on and be really careful of snakes." Snakes?!

What he should have said is that we actually needed to be careful of the huge bats, which were everywhere once we got inside. Walking carefully through the cave, we waved off bats and kept a sharp eye out for venomous snakes, but where were we going? The suspense was killing me, so I finally asked the chief. He said we were going to visit the head chief. I couldn't believe that the head chief lived in this cave, but he assured me that he did.

drua canoes

A distinct symbol of Fiji, the drua represents the finest and largest seagoing vessel ever crafted by the islanders. Measuring up to 93 feet long, these double-hulled, plank-built sailboats carried more than 200 people. Propelled by a large triangular sail, they were steered by a massive paddle operated by several people. The ingenious symmetric U-shaped profile of the craft meant the stern could transform into the bow and vice versa to keep wind in the sail.

The darkness enveloped us as we went so that I couldn't see anything unless the light from my headlamp was directly on it. I couldn't even see my hand in front of my face unless it fell into the beam of light. I was so focused on watching where I was walking that I didn't realize the chief had already stopped.

"I'd like you to meet the head chief," he announced. I stopped quickly, the light on my hat following the movement of my head as it whipped up. It flashed across a big, traditional Fijian canoe—called a drua—a large wood-carved vessel. But there wasn't just the canoe—there was also a complete skeleton. The bones were massive! I was sure that in his lifetime, this man had been some kind of war hero. And it was then that I realized that the head chief he was leading us to wasn't alive.

The chief became very solemn, kneeled down by the head chief, and began to tell us the story of his people. He told us that the chief we were looking at used to be the great chief of the people of this island, and they would battle with people from neighboring islands.

Many years ago, the head chief was out with his eight warriors on another island, and he was killed by the other island's chief. In ancient Fijian culture, if you kill someone's chief and eat them, then you get their people and their land. But if the chief's people can take his body and protect it so that the enemy islanders can't find it, then they can't take the people or the land.

Terrified they would lose their land and their tribe, his eight warriors bravely stole their head chief's lifeless body. They rushed him in their canoe to this cave, placing him as far back they could to hide him. Then they guarded him until each of them starved to death protecting their chief's body.

The chief shined his light next to the canoe and there they were—eight more skeletons. I shivered, feeling the power of the story and the sacrifice of all of the warriors. Because of that moment in their tribe's history, the chief and his people still exist on the island today. The chief's children had listened to this story, as riveted and affected as I was. This was their history, their legacy. Would the power to walk on fire still be theirs after all this time, too?

We said one last blessing before walking out of the cave, and at that point, we were all so hungry that I didn't even care about fire walking. The chief took us up the mountain again, over the rocks and through the jungle. We gathered coconuts and cassava. I was amazed how his children so easily shimmied up the trees, dropping coconuts down to us. I helped gather the cassava, pulling the roots, harvesting them, and then replanting them. As the chief explained to me, if you don't replant, you don't have crops.

Halfway through the harvest, I began to notice that we were collecting a lot of food—way more than we were going to need. When I mentioned this to the chief, he winked at me and said, "Well, if there's going to be fire walking, there needs to be a feast!"

cassava

Although the exact origins of cassava (*Manihot esculenta*) remain unknown, many believe it came from central Brazil. Domesticated in the Amazon between 7,000 and 9,000 years ago, it's now cultivated throughout the tropics where Pacific island diets, like those of the Fijians, have historically eaten root crops. Cassava (or tapioca) is one of the most popular staple crops in Fiji; boiled with salt and water until soft, it's eaten with curries and stews.

Fire walking? Finally! I wasn't sure what had convinced the chief to bring the ancient art back after 20 years—maybe he was feeling nostalgic or maybe he wanted to show me the ways of their tribe or maybe it was a way for him to honor the people who had made his life and the lives of his people possible. Whatever the reason, we were about to resurrect the first fire walking ceremony in decades.

We made a huge meal for the village with the food we'd collected, and the chief showed me how they prepared the rocks for fire walking. The men from the village brought in logs and stacked them to create a sort of Lincoln log type of cabin. And then they set it on fire.

I was curious why there was a hollow space in the middle of the logs, and the chief explained that that's where they cook the bodies they are going to eat. Um, were we going to eat someone? But the chief said, no, that this was just the traditional way to make a fire before a fire walk.

The fire burned all day while we feasted. When it was finally time for the fire walking, the men came running out of the jungle in grass skirts, bare chested and slathered in coconut oil and with dark charcoal markings and leaf head dresses. They began chanting as a light rain misted and the evening darkness crept in. We all stood around the fire to watch, enchanted in this moment. There was no sense of time—we could have been back in the time of their ancestors watching them prepare for a fire walking ritual.

The men pulled away the logs, dragging them onto the sand. The now exposed rocks were really hot, still flaming with the wooden embers of the timber that had been burning on them all day. We gathered around them and said a prayer. While some people still pounded on the drums and chanted, every single man that was there from the village took his turn walking on the fire. I had expected the atmosphere to be celebratory, but it was, in fact, quite somber.

The chief's turn came. He took a few steps onto the rocks then stopped and stood on them, flames licking up everywhere. The moment was surreal as he stood there, the flickering light of the fire playing across his face. It was an incredible thing to see him coming into himself, being a strong warrior of his people.

After he finished walking across the rocks, I immediately ran and grabbed his foot. I had to see his feet—they weren't even warm! I was absolutely amazed. The children were wide-eyed with amazement, too. It was time for the magic to be passed on to the next generation of fire walkers.

As we gathered around the dying embers, the chief kneeled down, a faraway look in his eyes, and shared how his tribe had received their fire walking power. He told the story of the fisherman and the eel—the one the ancient chief had spared that granted them the power to walk on fire and heal with touch. It was the legend that had drawn me on this quest.

As he finished the story, I thought back on everything I'd heard and been a part of since I'd come to this island—the restoring of natural resources, the sharing of stories, the respect for their rich history passed from generation to generation—and I think I understood better what the magic was really all about.

I'd come to this island on a quest to experience and understand fire walking. Now, having become accepted among the people of this island enough to be witness to a sacred piece of their history, I felt like a part of their magic had been shared with me.

And I carry it with me still.

CHAPTER NINE

TRASH ISLAND

Imagine being stranded on a remote island in the middle of the Indian Ocean for almost a month with a stranger you've never met with NOTHING, not even clothing. The 21 days I spent surviving the first season of Discovery Channel's *Naked and Afraid* changed the course of my life and led me to dive even deeper into defending and protecting our world waters.

It was the most challenging survival show in the history of TV, and I couldn't wait to put to the test the survival skills I'd learned growing up in cultures all over the world. Our location: a tiny island right above the equator in the Maldives.

With record-setting oppressive heat and a few coconuts to share, we were up against incredible odds. A human body can only survive four days without water and about three weeks without food. We needed to drink and eat to survive, so I went to work, quickly weaving a net from palm leaves to catch fish.

Desperate to catch us something to eat, I cast out my net and waited breathlessly to see what I pulled back in. As I reeled it back toward me, my stomach growling in anticipation, I could see that it was definitely full. But serious disappointment set in when I saw what it was full of— plastic. All shapes, sizes, and colors.

Where was all this plastic coming from? As I discovered, it travels from all over the world on ocean currents and ends up in all kinds of places, including remote islands in the Maldives. All this plastic is not only polluting our oceans; it's suffocating the ocean plants that provide most of our oxygen and killing many marine animals who mistake it for food. Plastic in the sea or rivers does not disappear. Instead, it releases deadly toxins and breaks down into small pieces called microplastics that fish eat and then we eventually ingest when we eat seafood. Not good.

I easily collected enough plastic bottles during our survival challenge that I was able to fashion them into clothing and a raft to reach our extraction point on the last day. Once safe on shore with the villagers admiring my raft, I questioned the locals about the plastic issue. I was shocked to learn that all 1,200 islands of the Maldives were covered in plastic, but many were cleaned daily for tourism.

When I asked them where all the collected plastic was taken, they told me about Trash Island. I had heard rumor of this island of plastic in the middle of the ocean. Was it possible that it actually existed? The sheer amount of discarded plastic on our little island made a big impression on me, but knowing that this was an even larger problem made me take up the cause and find ways to make things better.

stats on plastic pollution

Did you know that one million plastic drink bottles get sold every minute around the world? Or that another million plastic bags are used in those same 60 seconds? Yet, 91 percent of this plastic waste is single-use and never gets recycled. Burning it creates toxins that harm humans and animals, and so much of it—about eight million metric tons—finds its way into our oceans each year.

Introducing this waste into our oceans doesn't come without scary consequences. By 2050, plastic waste in our oceans will outweigh fish pound for pound. What's more, marine life and coral reef systems are dying at an alarming rate, which spells major trouble for plants and animals alike. Why? Because ocean plants generate 70 percent of the Earth's oxygen. Plastic chemicals such as BPA also prove dangerous to human beings when absorbed by the body. Today, 93 percent of Americans age six or older test positive for BPA.

While the show soared to number one and people were talking about *Naked and Afraid* everywhere, no one really wanted to talk about what I wanted to talk about—the plastic problem. How was I going to break through and get people to understand? An idea struck me. If I could document Trash Island, which I wasn't sure had been done before, and show the reality of what is happening through one of my short films, maybe I could raise enough awareness to make a change.

I set out for the Maldives once again—this time to visit Trash Island to see for myself just how large the plastic problem had become. When I arrived, I felt like I was in *Wall-E* or some crazy Transformers movie, where it's just mound after mound of plastic and burning waste and big, poofy, dark clouds of smoke. The smell was a completely overwhelming scent of trash and smog. You could smell and almost feel the toxicity of the smoke coming from the burning plastics.

small ways to make a big change

Plastic waste is a big problem. But it's one that we can combat through small, daily changes to our routine. Here are six ways to have a huge impact when it comes to getting rid of plastic and keeping our oceans and planet safe and pollution-free:

1. Use a reusable steel or wooden lunchbox.

2. When it comes to a water bottle, go for steel or glass that can be reused, too.

3. Remind your family to bring reusable bags when you go shopping for groceries and other items.

4. Just say no to polystyrene cups, plastic straws, and plastic stirrers.

5. Drink your hot cocoa out of reusable coffee and tea mugs, and remind your parents to do the same with their hot beverages.

6. When attending concerts and outdoor events, bring your own reusable cups.

When it's all said and done, the number one way to fight plastic pollution is by refusing single-use plastic. It's that simple.

Wandering around the island in my woven coconut hat with my pink surfboard made from recycled coffee cups, I looked for someone, anyone, to talk to about what was going on here. Finally, through the billows of smoke, a man emerged. He looked at me in both shock and amusement—I don't think he expected to see anyone, especially not a surfer girl.

He was happy to take a break and talk with me. I found out that Rajeesh lives and works on Trash Island, supervising everything. Through bits of broken English, I asked him about recycling, but he thought I was talking about cycling, as in bikes. He didn't seem to know anything about recycling.

I tried asking again about the plastics. This time he walked me over to where the plastic is kept, and my jaw dropped. It was like the Mount Everest of plastic. I just stood there in total awe of the sheer volume of plastic before me. Shampoo bottles, beach chairs, brooms, toothbrushes, bottles, straws, you name it. Anything that you can imagine that's plastic from every country in the world had come here to die and destroy paradise.

Not only are there mountains and mountains of it, but they're also burning it! That causes an even more severe issue—the release of deadly toxins into the air. And the worst part was that this cloud of toxic smoke regularly flowed right into the country's capital city, Malé, where a third of its population lives. I shuddered to think about what those toxic fumes could mean for the health of the people in the Maldives.

All I could think about was how to fix the problem, how to get recycling started in the Maldives, how to make reusable items out of all that plastic, how to get people to stop making plastic. There wasn't much I could do in that moment, but seeing the redness of his eyes from all the smoke, I gave Rajeesh my sunglasses. It was the only thing I had on me that I could think of that would potentially protect him at all. He was all smiles and told me how much he liked them.

With the sun beginning to set and the firelight from the plastic fires lighting our way, I said good-bye to Rajeesh. Knowing it wouldn't truly help but unable to bear leaving this island as it was, I took a bag of plastic with me, hoping to make a difference, however small it might be.

the "5 gyres" in the ocean where trash gathers

Did you know the ocean contains massive garbage patches where plastic pollution collects? The location of these patches is dictated by gyres, or large systems of circulating ocean currents. Think of them like slow-moving whirlpools. Gyres help circulate ocean waters around the globe. But they inadvertently draw in marine garbage, such as plastic pollution, too.

Where are these gyres and their associated garbage patches found? The five trash hotspots include: The North Atlantic Gyre, The South Atlantic Gyre, The North Pacific Gyre, The South Pacific Gyre, and The Indian Ocean Gyre.

The most infamous of these oceanic garbage patches remains the Great Pacific Garbage Patch, located in the North Pacific Gyre between Hawaii and California. But all of these gyres collect debris, which can circulate in the ocean for years, posing health threats to seabirds, marine animals, and fish.

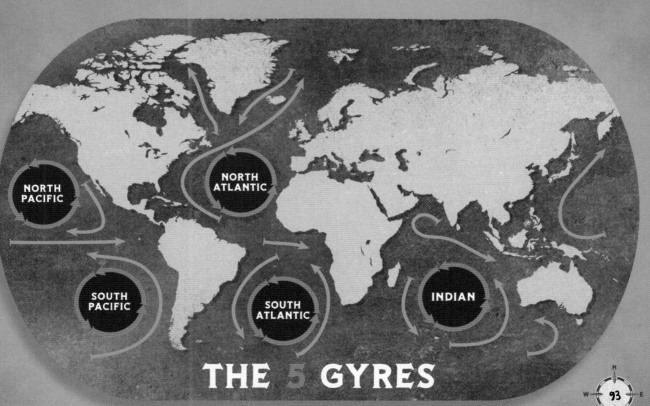

NORTH
PACIFIC

NORTH
ATLANTIC

SOUTH
PACIFIC

SOUTH
ATLANTIC

INDIAN

THE 5 GYRES

Upon returning to Hawaii, my story about Trash Island went viral. Before I could follow through on my plans for the little bag of plastic, people began to come to me from all over, moved by the story and wanting to help. I started working with the people of the Maldives to initiate the cleanup of Trash Island and put measures in place to protect this paradise I'd fallen in love with. Those measures are still in place today and are becoming models for other parts of the world with similar problems.

In the years that have followed, I've made it my mission to make a difference. I don't know all the answers—I'm just one person who wants to save our world waters. There are things we can all do to help—recycle, purchase reusable items made out of recycled materials, and find alternatives to plastic. But the most important is working with local and global organizations to pass laws against plastics, especially single-use plastics.

I'm proud to say that my films and photos have raised global awareness and have been instrumental in changing environmental laws. I helped get a law passed to ban plastic bags in California after paddling through the waters in Los Angeles when they were full of trash.

Also, in my home state of Hawaii, the reefs have been dying—we've lost nearly 50 percent of our reefs since 2011 due to pollutants like plastic and the toxins in most daily sunscreens. I worked to change legislation regarding sunscreens, and now toxic sunscreens are banned in our state.

As I continue my adventures, I've come to realize that this problem isn't just in the Maldives. Or Hawaii. Or even Los Angeles. Everywhere has their trash island. But if everybody makes little changes every day, if we work together, we can all make a big difference. Like my little bag of bottles from the island—with a little recycling magic, they are now one of my favorite pink bikinis!

Maldives

Los Angeles, California

CHAPTER TEN

SKELETONS OF THE UNDERWORLD

There are so many stories about time travel—people dream of venturing forward to see the incredible things that might be created in the future or back in time to see how the dinosaurs lived. With the help of some friends, I actually traveled back through time. Well, more like swam. Let me explain.

Four thousand years ago, the Mayans revered an amazing system of underwater caves, believing they were portals to the underworld. They built their villages around these divine pools of water, called cenotes (which means "sacred well"), and believed that through them they could speak to the gods.

Two million years before the Mayans, these same caves were dry. During the Ice Age, humans explored these caves, using them for shelter, as well as for burials. When the Ice Age ended just over 10,000 years ago, the ice melted, raising sea levels and flooding these caves. The beautiful cenotes of the Mayans and today were formed, but the homes and the people who had lived there have long since been submerged, lost to time and a change in climate.

How do we know all this? Time travel? Well, more like archaeology. In 1993, explorers made a history-altering discovery in one of the cenotes. They found the skeletal remains of a woman more than 10,000 years old. In 2004, Jeronimo Aviles extracted the remains. Jeronimo is part of a team of scientists that have been studying 10 prehistoric humans found deep inside the cenotes, including the 10,000-year-old woman, known as La Señora de las Palmas, or The Lady of the Palms.

Fascinated by both the history and the sacred water, I found myself trekking through the thick jungles of the Yucatán Peninsula to Jeronimo's lab at the Instituto de la Prehistoria de America to learn from the expert cave diver and researcher himself. Jeronimo's lab was filled with skeletons of prehistoric animals like giant sloths and sabertooth cats. It was like going back in time, *Jurassic Park* style!

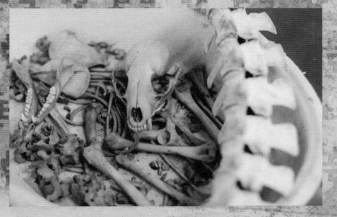

Jeronimo showed me an incredibly tiny ear bone he had found on the floor of one of the caves. Looking at it under a microscope, I wondered how he ever found something so small in a dark cave underwater. He explained that it was from one of the oldest humans ever discovered in the Americas. I felt that familiar tingle up my spine—this was amazing! Being a certified diver myself, I had to know what it was like to dive in the cenotes. How did they uncover these prehistoric bones? How did they collect them? Jeronimo, who was also a certified cave diving instructor, agreed to show me.

The cenotes are all over the Yucatán, but there are many clustered near Tulum, which is where we went. They are also interconnected with tunnels that can be quite narrow, with only enough room for a diver with an air tank, that lead to enormous chambers. Some of the tunnels go out into the ocean, some lead to other cenotes. There are even tunnels in very remote locations.

The cenote we visited was known by Jeronimo and his team as The Cemetery. To get there, we trekked deep into the dense, humid jungle, carrying twice our weight in scuba gear. Afraid of getting swallowed up by the thick vegetation and becoming hopelessly lost, I followed right on Jeronimo's heels. He stopped suddenly, preventing me from taking one more step and falling into a deep hole I hadn't seen coming.

Peering over the edge, I could see it was a cenote! The opening was high above the water and draped by bright green vines, the water shimmering a surreal blue a good distance down. Seeing no obvious entrance other than this hole in the ground, I asked him how we would get in.

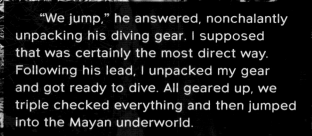

"We jump," he answered, nonchalantly unpacking his diving gear. I supposed that was certainly the most direct way. Following his lead, I unpacked my gear and got ready to dive. All geared up, we triple checked everything and then jumped into the Mayan underworld.

After getting into the water, we placed our tanks on a rock ledge and decided to acclimate to the water with a free dive. Jeronimo gave me some tips on the differences between the kind of ocean diving I was used to and diving in caves. He stressed how dangerous these dives could be, because some of the areas are very, very tight. Also, the way in which you use your fins is different, so that you don't kick up the very fine sediment on the bottom. If it mixes with the water, we won't be able to see anything, and by the time it settled, our tanks would be dry. And we would be dead. I took his advice very seriously.

cavern and cave diving in the yucatán peninsula

The cenotes of Yucatán, Mexico, contain countless unexplored mysteries. For the scuba divers who explore their submerged depths, cenotes can feel like entering an alternate world—one of overhangs, stalactites, stalagmites, and ancient treasures. Known as cavern diving, divers are never more than 131 feet away from the cenote's surface. This makes for splendid views of the sun's rays filtering down through the depths of the pool.

Beneath the cenotes, you'll find intricate networks of caves like the roots of a tree. Scuba divers also explore these water-filled depths where no light can penetrate. Cavern diving at cenotes requires little more than a flashlight and regular scuba gear, but cave diving comes with a variety of specific equipment. You'll also need plenty of training and experience because of the dangers associated with this activity.

Even with Jeronimo's dire warnings in the back of my mind, I couldn't help but be taken in by the beauty of the cenote. It was a little otherworldly. The rays of light coming into the cave and shining down through the water look almost fake when you're underwater with the darkness of the cave around you and this bright, watery beam lighting up that single space.

I followed Jeronimo's every move as we descended down, following the light ray into the depths. Strange fish that looked like miniature sharks darted in and out of the light beam. It was silent, spooky, and seemingly bottomless. At the same time, it felt liberating to be diving through such a pristine light beam hugged by intense darkness. It was impossible to reach the bottom on a free dive, and as I glided back up the prism of light, I felt like I was being abducted by aliens to another planet.

Confident that I was ready for our expedition into the watery grave, Jeronimo reminded me of the most important thing to keep in sight: the line (which looked more like a thin thread). It was set before we started our dive, which all cave divers should do. When exploring a new cave, divers set lines like scientific breadcrumbs to make sure they don't get lost in the maze of cave systems. It's truly been a lifesaver. Sometimes, divers can be underwater for an entire day, hiding air tanks along the route for additional oxygen and relying on the lines to find their way back out.

Now armed with my dive gear and flashlights (on my head and in my hand), we descended into the cenote again, but this time not in the light beam. I didn't know it at that moment, but this was also my journey back in time.

As we left the light from the surface behind, I was glad for the flashlights illuminating the darkness around us. After diving down into the seemingly endless dark, our lights revealed the cave floor. Jeronimo turned hard right and pointed at the opening of a tiny tunnel. We were supposed to go through there? There was no way we would fit!

But Jeronimo motioned for me to follow him through the small passage. Our powerful dive lights reflected off of the close cave walls, illuminating the entire passage. My jaw dropped, or it would have if my lips were not clinging so hard to my air regulator. It was stunning and terrifying all at once. Massive sharp stalactites and stalagmites dripped from the ceiling and jutted up from the cave floor.

I remember Jeronimo telling me, whatever you do, do not bump into these prehistoric formations because not only are they valuable to geology and the preservation of the caves, but also they are like sharp spears that can penetrate you or worse— collapse a portion or even all of the fragile cave. My heart pounding in my ears, it took every ounce of grace I could muster with my clunky tanks to follow Jeronimo single file, weaving in and out of natural booby traps.

As we rounded a corner, the chamber widened and Jeronimo shone his light on a ledge in front of us. On the ancient altar-like formation was a skull with light beams streaming through its eyes from our lights. Wow! It was an Indiana Jones moment of a lifetime. It appeared perfectly preserved after more than 10,000 years. I was awe-struck.

As if it was just another day at the office for Jeronimo, he swam to the skull and took out an underwater notepad and measuring stick. Careful not to touch it, he demonstrated for me how they log information when they make new discoveries like this. With the data he collected, he could return with his team to do a proper extraction of the skull.

I was so excited about our discovery that I didn't realize I had resorted to the wrong kind of kicking. Sediment swarmed up around me until I was encapsulated in darkness. I panicked, looking for Jeronimo's light. Nothing. Little particles swirled around me, and within seconds I was completely disoriented.

Looking down to check my air gauge, I discovered that I couldn't even see it inches from my face. The worst thoughts imaginable flooded my head. Just as I was wondering if I'd be the next skeleton on the cenote floor, Jeronimo's hand came through the sediment, grabbed my arm, and guided my hand to a line. We had to be inches from each other but still couldn't see each other. I followed along the line as he had taught me, and a few moments later, we came out of the sediment into another cavern with a light ray shining down from above. He gave me an "Are you OK?" signal. I shakily signaled back "OK."

We ascended the line near the light ray, stopping at increments as required in scuba to decompress our lungs (and for me to calm my nerves). On those stops, Jeronimo pointed out bone fragments of giant sloths, prehistoric pigs, and sabertooth cats on surrounding ledges. We were literally swimming through a time machine.

But our escape from the silt had taken us back a different way than we'd come. Jeronimo led us through a different cenote. As mystical an experience as it was down in the caves themselves, coming up to the surface of this cenote was a rather shocking experience. There was plastic and trash as far as the eye could see.

how cenotes form

Despite the lush jungles of the Yucatán Peninsula of northern Mexico, few surface rivers or streams punctuate the flat land. Fortunately, cenotes provide stable freshwater sources for animals and humans. Limestone sinkholes filled with water, cenotes take thousands of years to make. How are they formed? When rainwater absorbs carbon dioxide from the atmosphere, it creates a weak acid. This trickles down through cracks in the limestone dissolving calcite in the rock and breaking up the limestone. Over time, a large underground cavern emerges with a thin limestone roof. When this roof collapses, it leaves a water-filled hole.

Dismayed at the sight of it all, Jeronimo told me that this is a large problem for the cenotes. Even deeper in the jungle, there is trash and plastic. It might have been dumped there, but it also travels on the ocean currents in the caves and can be anywhere in any cenote. I was so shocked that in the days to come, I set off on my surfboards to see the extent of the plastic pollution plaguing the Yucatán Peninsula.

Whether the plastic is actually in the water or on the ground, the toxins are getting into the water. Whenever it rains and then the sun beats down on this plastic, it releases toxins. Mixed with the rainwater, the toxins easily pass through the porous limestone into the water.

And as more and more people visit these cenotes and the areas around them are developed, the problem is only increasing. Ancient humans had been wiped out by climate change before the Mayans, and the Mayans disappeared as well. As the theory goes, if we don't make a change, we could become extinct, too. We're inducing environmental changes with all the plastic waste piling up out of sight and out of mind in places like the cenotes.

sam meacham's freshwater stats

Imagine jumping on a rocket ship and heading into outer space. You'd marvel at the tranquil beauty of our green-and-blue-colored planet. The blue hue comes from water, which covers 75 percent of the Earth's surface. Yet, if all of the Earth's water was collected in one spot, it would fill a sphere no bigger than 858 miles in diameter. That's the distance between Mexico City and Cancún.

Much of this water can't be consumed by human beings because freshwater only accounts for about 3 percent of the water on Earth. This miniscule amount would create a sphere 168 miles in diameter and fit nicely atop the Yucatán Peninsula. Of this much smaller amount, only 0.65 percent is available for human consumption. In other words, humans derive 80 percent of their drinking water from a volume of liquid that could fit in a ball 35 miles in diameter. That's the distance between Cancún and Playa del Carmen.

The first step is being aware. The second is to start making changes. Both of these things are already underway, but it makes me wish that there really was a way to travel through time to go forward and see how well our current efforts worked. Or, better yet, to go back and prevent the problem from happening in the first place. But since that can't happen, I'll settle for helping as much as I can.

I've teamed up with an expert on cave diving, the Yucatán, and our most precious natural resource—water. Sam Meacham heads up CINDAQ, an organization dedicated to research, education, and the conservation of natural and cultural resources, specifically for the cenotes. Working with Sam and CINDAQ, we're striving to make some positive changes for the future of the cenotes and the underground rivers connecting them.

Exploring the cenotes, finding prehistoric artifacts, and seeing their incredible beauty and importance has only solidified in my mind what a treasure these waters are to us and how much I hope they're preserved for the enjoyment of future generations.

CHAPTER ELEVEN

SURFING THE CATACOMBS

Underneath one of the most popular cities in the world there is a labyrinth of secret tunnels holding over six million skeletons. The Paris catacombs are also the location of some of the most pristine pools of clear, blue water. The chance for adventure AND promoting the protection of a freshwater source? Cue the Indiana Jones theme song. I grabbed my pink surfboard and headed to France.

Also known as the world's largest grave, the catacombs are actually ancient mines where rocks were extracted to construct the city of Paris, France. When the city's cemeteries began to become too full, they removed the bodies and transferred them to large caverns within the mines. The maze of tunnels spans more than 200 miles, and one wrong turn could leave you lost in the underworld forever.

There are parts of the catacombs that are open to tourists, where you can go on a guided tour of some of the more well-known areas. But a large part of the catacombs is unknown and unmapped, and few dare to venture into the seemingly forbidden territory for fear of being lost forever.

There are three levels to the catacombs, and it's said that on the lowest level there are beautiful blue pools of water deep underground. I wanted to document them and bring attention to the importance of protecting freshwater sources like these. Because if your underground water gets polluted, where are you going to get clean water from?

My catacomb adventure started late one evening after the sun had already set. I met my guides and we set off, going down and down and down until we were far below ground. I didn't speak a lot of French and they didn't speak a lot of English, so I had no idea where we were going. This was definitely an exercise in trust! They handed me an ancient-looking lantern with an actual flame and hand motioned for me to stay close to them. They had spent years exploring the catacombs, and because they were also passionate about protecting the environment, they were happy to help me in my quest.

We were too far down for our cell phones to get signals, and none of us had a watch on. With darkness pressing down on us from all sides, it was hard to tell what time of day it might have been or how quickly time was passing. I hadn't quite known what to expect, but the lack of sound was unsettling to me. It was hard to believe that the hustle and bustle of Paris was above us while down here it felt like the underworld—a sound vacuum where no matter how loud I yelled, no one would hear me. The dirt and stone walls around us absorbed it all.

With our lanterns casting shadows on the jagged edges of the rocks all around us, I couldn't shake the feeling that there was always someone behind me. I found it hard to breathe, and not just because of my nerves. There was a distinct lack of oxygen this far below ground. But the sense of moving forward to escape whatever doom was nipping at my heels kept me right behind my guides as we forged ahead.

I'm not sure how long it took, but we arrived at the first tunnel with water. This wasn't the pristine water I'd come to see—you have to go through some muddier water before it becomes clear. But my surfboard came in handy, and I started paddling through the water, enjoying a little time "surfing" the catacombs.

pools beneath catacombs

Many people don't realize the Parisian Catacombs also boast crystal-clear blue pools. These hidden swimming pools remain one of Paris's best-kept secrets. They represent the summer playground of cataphiles (urban explorers who tour the Parisian Catacombs). Off-limits to the general public, the watery tunnels remain largely unmapped.

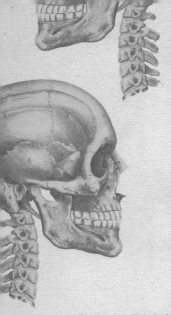

What we didn't know at the time was that it was pouring rain above ground, which affects the water table below ground. The water began to rise rapidly. I hadn't planned ahead—none of my gear was waterproof. I used my surfboard to carry our things to keep them as dry as possible, but the water kept rising, first at my waist, then my chest, and then my chin. I quickly realized we were going to have to go all the way under!

I gasped to grab a last breath of air before the water flooded over my head. Clinging to the leash of my surfboard, I dove down and swam as strong as I could up the tunnel. It felt like the terrifying and iconic moment from *Titanic* where the water rises and Jack and Rose have to hold their breaths until they can swim to a chamber with air.

I tried to calm my mind and focus on swimming, but I'd been under for a while and I needed air. My body began to convulse. Instinctively, I bolted for the surface, though I expected to bump into the ceiling. Instead, I actually popped up into a few inches of air! Somehow, my headlamp was still dimly shining. With it I could see that there was a dry chamber in the distance.

Fortunately for us, we had been swimming uphill through the chamber, and right when I thought we were doomed, there was now space between the top of the water and the roof of the tunnel. Finding our footing as the water became more shallow, we rushed through the tunnel, desperate to get to higher ground. The maze of tunnels had narrowed, and it appeared there was only one tunnel to get out. It was so small and tight that we had to slither on our stomachs to get through to it. At that point, I wasn't sure if my guides even knew where we were, but we all knew one thing—we could not go back the way we came.

Everything we had was soaked, and we were freezing. Able to stand up again, mud squished between my bare toes as we moved up to what we hoped was a dryer area. Most of our lighting had gone out in the water. My headlamp was still working, lighting my way forward. I kept focused on it, because everything else was pitch dark. I noticed the mud had dried, but then I suddenly heard crunching under my feet. Creeped out because I had no idea what I was stepping on, I dropped my head so that my lamp shone on the floor beneath me, and I nearly jumped out of my skin. Bones. We were walking on an endless amount of human bones.

a parade of skeletons

Thousands of years of human occupation in Paris have led to periods of serious overcrowding at city cemeteries. By 1786, the problem of where to place the dead reached a breaking point. The cemetery of Saints-Innocents flooded, sending dead bodies into neighboring buildings. In response, civic leaders started relocating millions of skeletons from the city's cemeteries. Where? To nearly 200 miles of tunnels, known as the Catacombs, located beneath the City of Lights.

The Catacombs were dug by medieval and Renaissance miners who tunneled beneath the city in search of limestone and gypsum—the very building blocks of the city. But these tunnels soon provided the perfect spot for Paris's dearly departed. During the French Revolution, the deceased were buried directly in the Catacombs' ossuaries. This practice ended in 1860. But you can still tour the skeleton parade for yourself on a journey through Paris's underground tunnels.

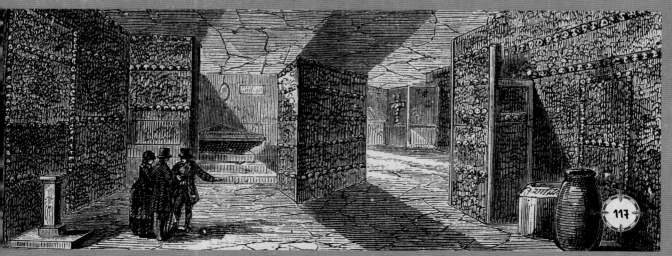

I called out to my guides—I couldn't possibly walk over this. These bones had once been people! My guides were practical. This was the only way out. Either walk over the bones or drown.

Saying prayers for those that these bones had belonged to and trying to be as respectful as possible, we walked over them on our way to safety. I did my best to straddle the walls whenever possible, lifting myself over the bones so that there was a minimum of disturbance to them, hoping that someday they would all be laid to a proper rest.

fare bones art

The Catacombs hold the remains of approximately six million Parisians. Most of the bones were transferred from the city's cemeteries between 1787 and 1814. Workers piled them in quarries without much thought. But France's Emperor Napoleon changed all of that. He decided to transform Paris's subterranean depths into a tourist attraction on par with Rome's Catacombs. He appointed workers to turn the labyrinth of bone-filled tunnels into something the people would want to see. Workers rearranged the haphazardly placed bones into elaborate patterns, including skulls and crossbones, circles, hearts, and crosses.

I thought that the rain had ruined our quest, but I was wrong. On our way to safety, we passed a magnificent freshwater pool! We were able to take pictures and document the beauty of these amazing underground natural resources. I would have loved to have had more time here, but we couldn't take the chance that the floodwaters would continue to rise and trap or drown us down here.

The way out ended up being a storm drain. We had to tie a rope to my surfboard to lift it up, but my guides, our gear, and I made it out of the catacombs. I had never been so glad to breathe fresh air!

Much like the city of Paris itself, the catacombs exude a sense of magic, mystery, and romance. Its miles of hidden tunnels and chambers contain dangers and secrets—it's alluring and exciting, but it's also to be respected. It's a sacred place with equal amounts of beauty and peril. It's a place worth protecting and preserving.

CHAPTER TWELVE

THE GREATEST TREASURE ON EARTH

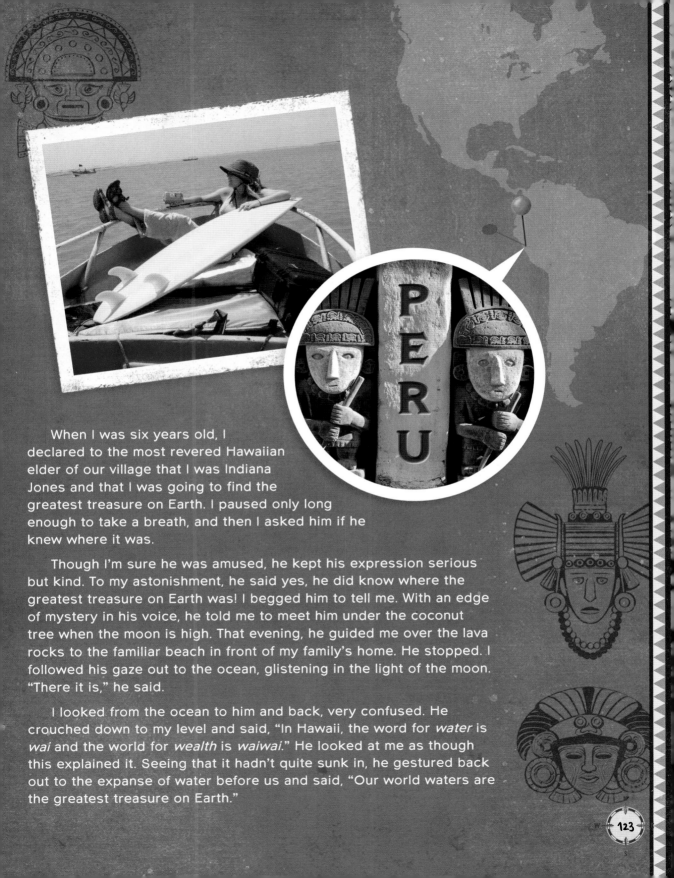

When I was six years old, I declared to the most revered Hawaiian elder of our village that I was Indiana Jones and that I was going to find the greatest treasure on Earth. I paused only long enough to take a breath, and then I asked him if he knew where it was.

Though I'm sure he was amused, he kept his expression serious but kind. To my astonishment, he said yes, he did know where the greatest treasure on Earth was! I begged him to tell me. With an edge of mystery in his voice, he told me to meet him under the coconut tree when the moon is high. That evening, he guided me over the lava rocks to the familiar beach in front of my family's home. He stopped. I followed his gaze out to the ocean, glistening in the light of the moon. "There it is," he said.

I looked from the ocean to him and back, very confused. He crouched down to my level and said, "In Hawaii, the word for *water* is *wai* and the world for *wealth* is *waiwai*." He looked at me as though this explained it. Seeing that it hadn't quite sunk in, he gestured back out to the expanse of water before us and said, "Our world waters are the greatest treasure on Earth."

It took time to process that. I didn't fully appreciate it at age six, but it's become a part of who I am and what I'm passionate about. After film school, I knew I wanted to bring my biggest interests into a film series—surfing, protecting the oceans, and uncovering treasures. Of course, I still wanted to be Indiana Jones, too! So where better to start than one of the ultimate locations for adventure—Peru!

With the rich history of the Incans, Machu Picchu, amazing ruins, and some of the best surfing in the world, Peru was the perfect place to go. I wanted to create an episode for my new film series that would combine surfing with a captivating adventure. My goal was to pass on the stories of ancient times before they are lost forever. I had no idea that this trip would be the catalyst for some wild coincidences and one bone-chilling discovery.

Arriving in Peru, I met up with Octopus—they call him Pulpo, which is Spanish for Octopus—a local legendary surf guide. Built more like a football player than a surfer, his dark eyes and mustache made him feel mysterious and a little intimidating, but I quickly found out that Octopus had a great sense of humor and a love for the ocean as big as mine. He was the perfect person to team up with.

We met on the Peruvian coastline, which was much more desolate than I had imagined. Here you'll find a desert of rugged terrain and rolling sand dunes dotted occasionally with a bush here and there. In rare sections of the coast where rivers flow to the sea, there are thick marshlands teeming with tall reeds and massive crocodiles. Not the friendliest of environments.

Undeterred, we set off with our surfboards, pulled along on Octopus's "Peruvian Ferrari," which was really a donkey pulling a two-wheeled cart. With his knowledge and expertise, we trekked through the inhospitable desert region to remote spots along the coast and surfed so many incredible breaks along the way. Peru is the "land of the lefts," and we got to surf the longest left-hand point break in the world. Peru's famous Chicama is such a long wave that at the end of the wave, you take a small motor taxi back to the beginning to do it all over again!

One evening as Octopus was scouting another secret surf spot for us, we sat down at the top of a sand dune to take a break and watch the sun dipping down over the vast ocean. I hadn't realized this kind of beauty existed in this barren environment. As we sat there, I felt something pricking the bottom of my leg. I reached down and picked up a little, white, shiny seashell. I showed it to Octopus, and his eyes became absolutely enormous.

He began shouting, "Comida de los Muertos!" which translates to "food of the dead." He was telling me that the little white shell I had been sitting on had been placed there as food for a dead person. As I looked around, I noticed more and more little white shells. Did that mean that someone was buried right beneath where I was sitting?

chicama, the longest wave

In northwestern Peru, you'll find a true surfer's paradise: the small coastal town of Puerto Chicama, home to the longest, most perfect wave on the planet. It stretches an impossible 1.4 miles from a cluster of rocks where the wave breaks to a desolate pier where it ends. According to locals, a skilled surfer in ideal conditions can catch and ride one wave the entire distance. That's a three- to five-minute ride—an eternity in the surfing world, where every second counts!

Immediately, I jumped up, and then he jumped up. Octopus explained that in ancient times, the pre-Incan people would bury their elite at the highest point near the ocean. Glancing around us, that's exactly where we were. Curious, Octopus and I began to gently brush away the sand.

Only inches beneath the surface, we uncovered a cloth. Underneath was the mummy of a 3,000-year-old pre-Incan chief. Over the centuries, the desert wind had blown away much of the sands covering this grave. A glint of gold caught my eye as the wind whipped the sand off of the chief's skull, revealing a gleaming gold nose piece. Octopus explained that the piece depicted what was called the Caballito de Totora, which is an ancient type of boat built with reeds that the pre-Incans would use a lot like a surfboard.

"He was a surfer," Octopus exclaimed with a smile.

We had uncovered a surfing chief! I couldn't believe it. Octopus went on to say that the pre-Incans were the first surfers in the world and would paddle out to fish and then catch waves on their way back to shore. Alongside the chief was a carved wooden paddle inlaid with precious stones, as well as a ceramic figurine in the shape of a "fisherman surfer" on the Caballito de Totora.

According to Octopus, the pre-Incans would bury their royalty with all kinds of memorabilia honoring the ocean, because they believed it to be the provider of life. Then they would sprinkle the tiny white shells over top of the grave to serve as food for the afterlife.

caballito de totora

For more than 3,000 years, Peruvian fishermen have used Caballitos de Totoras to surf the Pacific Ocean. These reed watercrafts help them navigate past the breakers where they lay fishing nets and drop traps for lobsters. When the Spanish first arrived in Peru in the 16th century, they gave the modern name to this ingenious cross between a boat and a surfboard. The word "caballito" means "little horse," and "totora" refers to the native reeds used to build it. Peruvian surfing originated in the coastal city of Huanchaco, as evidenced by thousands of pottery shards, rock art paintings, and other Chimú and Inca artifacts found in the area. They depict ancient people riding Caballitos de Totoras. These finds have caused a controversy in the surfing world about the true birthplace of surfing. Is it Hawaii or Peru? The debate continues, but one thing's for sure. Peru has produced some of the world's best surfers, including Felipe Pomar and Sofía Mulánovic, the only South American female athlete ever to be crowned world surfing champion.

I sat back and gazed on our discovery. It was an incredible moment, and I felt such a connection to this surfing chief I'd never known. What an amazing thing to know just how much this man and his people had revered the water. I had always wanted to share that our oceans are the greatest treasure on Earth, and here I was uncovering real buried treasure—and what was the message? The importance of the sea!

It's pretty powerful when you're Indiana Jones seeking treasure and the treasure that you find aligns with the treasure that you love. Everything was aligning. Not just the surfing, but the importance of world waters. The belief that water equals life. That water is our greatest treasure. It wasn't only me believing that—people on this Earth thousands of years before me knew it, too.

Discovering and understanding the ancient ways of people can help us keep our planet healthy and give us solutions we might never have thought of or at least a different way to look at things. Even surfing.

Respectfully recovering the mummy, we offered our blessings to the chief and his people. I looked out at the waves, trying to imagine what it would have been like to surf the Caballito de Totora. Octopus must have read my mind, because before I knew it, he swept us up and headed out to find some friends of his that he said could show us.

We made our way to one of the swampy areas. I followed Octopus, trudging through a thick marshland, up to our waists in water. It looked like a great home for snakes. As I began to wonder if the crocodiles were hungry, a machete came slicing through the reeds near my head. I leapt back, ready to make a run for it. The tall stalks parted, revealing a toothless, grinning older man carrying a bundle of reeds on one shoulder and a machete in the other hand. He rushed excitedly to embrace Octopus.

I came to learn that this man and his son were some of the last surviving descendants of the pre-Incans who still fished and surfed with the Caballito de Totora, which is exactly what he was making with the reeds he was chopping down with his machete. They agreed to take me surfing, pre-Incan style, and let me tell you, that's not the easiest thing in the world!

First, it took all of us just to get the "surfboard" in the water, and then when reed boats get wet, they get very heavy! My hat's off to the pre-Incans who mastered the use of them. I kept flipping over because there is no fin to stabilize the craft, and because they're made out of reeds, they got waterlogged quickly. And so did I!

chan chan, the coastal machu picchu

Peru is synonymous with the ancient Inca and their crowning achievement, Machu Picchu. But did you know that many other impressive Incan and pre-Incan sites still exist, too? These include Chan Chan, the largest city in pre-Columbian South America. Built on the northern coast of Peru in 850 A.D., Chan Chan remains emblematic of the pre-Incan Chimú culture.

The site covers nearly 14 square miles and contains nine citadels with storehouses, reservoirs, temples, and more. Archaeologists estimate Chan Chan once contained 10,000 structures (some with walls 30 feet high) and 40,000 to 60,000 people lived there before the Incas conquered it in the 15th century.

As my time with Octopus and my new Peruvian surfer friends came to an end over a dinner of fresh fish caught on the Caballito de Totora, I knew that I'd filmed a great story, and I couldn't wait to share it with the world. It was one of those moments in life where I could feel deep down that I was on the right path. I'd studied filmmaking because I'd wanted to make movies that entertain and inspire. By uncovering the mummy, I had uncovered the true heart and soul of what I wanted to share with my Alison's Adventures films— carrying on the legacy, the stories, the treasures. I hoped to leave my own legacy and be an inspiration to others.

Heading back home, I couldn't wait to share my incredible adventure with the Hawaiian elder and tell him that he was right about the greatest treasure on Earth. As soon as I got back, I went to visit him. Much older now and unable to walk very far, he still accompanied me to the ocean and we dove in. As we swam, he pointed out the lack of fish and the dead coral that had once been vibrant and healthy. Hawaii has lost almost 50 percent of its reef systems since 2011. Our treasure was dying.

I took up the cause to help Hawaii's reefs, making a film to show the devastation of the ecosystem due to toxic sunscreens. I wanted to create a ban on the use of them in Hawaii. The law recently passed! And so did my revered Hawaiian elder. Before he died, he asked me to pass on his stories to future generations so that they, too, could understand the importance of our greatest treasure and, like Indiana Jones, protect it.

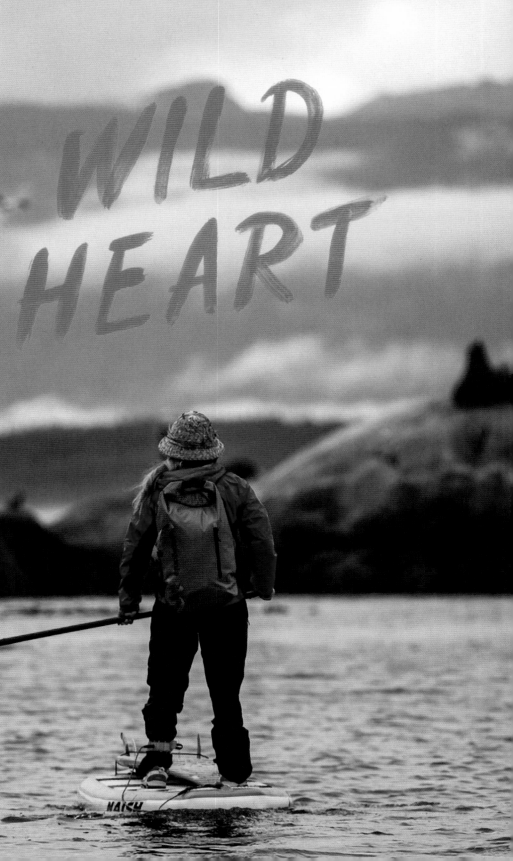

CHAPTER THIRTEEN

WILD
HEART

I've survived naked on an island for a month, swam with the largest sharks on Earth, and paddled up to erupting volcanoes—but for some unknown reason, my greatest fear is coming face-to-face with a grizzly bear. This is an animal with a bite force that could chomp through steel as if it were butter, and there have been 664 attacks on humans between 2000 and 2015. It's one of the most deadly animals in North America.

So, would I want to go out into the wilderness looking for one? Definitely not. But, somehow, that's exactly what I did.

This adventure started before I appeared on *Naked and Afraid*, during my last-minute crunch time preparing for the show. I only had a few days to prepare, and I spent that time at home in Hawaii practicing all the primitive skills I'd learned growing up in tribes around the world. But try as I might, I could not seem to master making fire by friction with tropical sticks. If I were to survive monsoon season near the equator, I would need fire.

Frustrated at my lack of success, I took a break, paddling my surfboard out to catch a wave and clear my mind. My distress must have shown on my face, because another surfer I didn't even know stopped to ask me if I was OK. Before I could even think, I just blurted out, "I can't make fire with sticks!" Realizing how ridiculous that must have sounded, I started to explain, but the woman excitedly responded, "That's my favorite thing to do!"

It turned out that this surfer was Nikki van Schyndel, one of the greatest survivalists in the world. She had come all the way from the forests of British Columbia, Canada, to learn how to surf. I was more than happy to teach her some of the finer points of surfing, and she was happy to help me learn how to make fire. We went into the Hawaiian wilderness, where we collected plants and rubbed together every kind of stick we could find until we finessed the perfect combination of tropical wood to make fire by friction.

Nikki and I swapped survival-skill secrets—hers from the forest, mine from the tropics. We were instant friends, and it was nice to have that extra girl-power support to solve a survival problem. Honestly, it was her overflowing positivity and confidence in me that helped carry me through my challenging month stranded in the Maldives.

When I left for the show, she told me that when I returned, I had to promise to visit her and her "grizzly friends" in British Columbia. It didn't dawn on me at the time that she wasn't talking about old hairy friends—she was talking about REAL grizzly bears! You see, Nikki is a bear whisperer. She first set out to spend a year and a half in the wilderness with nothing but a cat and a rowboat. She enjoyed it so much, she's spent more than 10 years in the Great Bear Rainforest.

great bear rainforest

One of the wildest places on Earth, the Great Bear Rainforest stretches for more than 250 miles along British Columbia's coast. It contains one of the last large expanses of temperate rainforest in the world. Indigenous or "First Nations" communities have protected this sacred land for thousands of years. Wildlife living in the region include sea otters, coastal gray wolves, cougars, grizzlies, and the white spirit bear—the rarest bear on the planet.

She's a survivalist, but she's also a nature lover. Nikki has come face-to-face with grizzly bears and lived to tell about it. Her belief is that if you respect them, they will respect you. I wasn't so convinced, but I couldn't pass up an adventure opportunity, so I kept my promise and set off for Nikki's island, which is known to be one of the most remote and difficult places to access. After days of planes and busses and ferries, I had to hitch a ride on a small, local fishing boat to make the final crossing.

After getting lost in the fog and nearly being forced to spend a freezing night on a boat, I finally made it to the island. I hopped onto land and wandered into the forest, suddenly realizing that I was in a seriously isolated area. There was no such thing as calling for help or any sort of "grizzly attack rescue" this far from civilization.

As I came to terms with the potential danger I'd placed myself in, I initially failed to notice the beauty of the British Columbian forests. It was a like a fairy land! The canopy that the trees created allowed prisms of light to shine through to the mossy forest floor. I consider myself to be very comfortable in nature, and while the beauty was alluring, the threat of grizzlies coming out of the brush around me was enough to make the forest feel more eerie than pretty.

So when a bush near me began to shake, I whirled around in a panic, terrified a grizzly had found me already. But it was Nikki who emerged from the bush, wearing a Davy Crockett–style coonskin hat and carrying a large, freshly caught salmon that was so big, I ended up hugging both Nikki and the fish when she rushed over to greet me.

survivalist training

Have you ever wondered what it takes to survive in the wilderness? Survivalist training courses provide the answers, teaching important skills necessary for navigating British Columbia's breathtaking yet unforgiving wilderness. During a course, students learn about shelter building, basic first aid, how to start a fire, how to build traps, and more. Bushcraft, a more intense form of survival training, relies on nature's resources, rather than humanmade equipment, to craft the tools necessary for survival.

I'd arrived in time for dinner. Nikki excitedly showed me which sticks were good for making fire, and we cooked salmon survival-style. While it spent endless hours cooking, Nikki collected a variety of plants, making a "bush stir-fry" side dish. It's truly incredible what's edible in the wild if you know what to look for. We enjoyed a meal of fresh salmon and "veggies," with a front-row view of the beautiful Canadian landscape. It was perhaps the best meal I'd ever had.

It got dark quickly, and we settled in for the night. And with the night came my nerves. Nikki decided to tell a "bedtime story" about a cougar that once cuddled with her for warmth. She'd woken with one tucked in beside her, an encounter she'll never forget. She said that they are one of Canada's most dangerous predators and to be aware in the night if one approaches. If I hadn't already been nervous, I was now nearly terrified to sleep.

I spent the whole night on edge, ready for a grizzly or a cougar to find me in my sleeping bag. I woke up clinging to both my flashlight and my survival knife, cuddling them like a teddy bear for comfort. Nikki was already up making a breakfast of berries and edible flowers. The dew sparkled in the morning sun, and after taking a gulp of the fresh forest air, I felt refueled. I scrambled out of my sleeping bag to help Nikki prep for our adventure.

The sounds of the forest echoed softly around us as we packed our cameras and supplies. Nikki's years of experience living with grizzly bears meant that we weren't bringing along any of the conventional precautions, like bear spray or weapons. While this left my heart beating a little rapidly, I completely trusted Nikki and was ready to move forward and face my fears. With the majesty of the forest surrounding us, we quietly set out on our quest.

grizzly bears

The largest of two bears found in British Columbia, grizzly bears (*Ursus arctos horribilis*) number about 15,000—25 percent of North America's entire population. They can easily weigh 800 pounds or more and tower 8 feet tall. Extremely fast over short distances, they're capable of bringing down moose, elk, or bison, making them one of nature's most formidable predators. Yet they prefer eating nuts, berries, leaves, fruit, and insects. Their favorite treat? Moths. Female grizzlies with cubs can be aggressive, as can bears looking for food. So it's important to secure food properly while camping and to make a lot of noise while hiking to avoid catching mothers with cubs off-guard.

Deeper in the woods, Nikki stopped suddenly and the hair went up on the back of my neck. She whispered softly, letting me know that from here on out we were in grizzly territory. We needed to be as silent as possible. If I stepped on a twig and made a noise, freeze. If she stopped, I stopped. If she gave me an instruction, I followed it. She said I should focus on becoming one with the forest. I was more focused on not becoming a grizzly bear's lunch, but I did my best to follow her instructions.

My heart was pounding in my chest. It felt like I stepped on everything that could possibly make noise. How were the bears not going to hear us coming? The woods were so thick, I could be inches from a great grizzly and not know it. With every move, I had no idea what might happen.

We were headed toward the river, and as we got close, Nikki motioned for me to stop. She disappeared for a few minutes. A few terrifying minutes. I heard a little whistle and saw Nikki down by the edge of the river. She motioned to me to join her. I dropped down to my knees and crawled quietly beside her. Peeking out over the log we were hiding behind, we watched as a massive grizzly bear came lumbering out of the forest on the other side of the river. He

Nikki quietly encouraged me to slow my heart rate because they can sense both fear and movement. I could sense a bit of fear in her voice because of my growing terror. "Just be like a tree," she calmly demanded. Great. My freak-out was going to get us eaten. I had no idea how to slow my heartbeat with a large grizzly bear moving our way!

I kept telling myself to be like a tree. *Be like a tree. I'm going to die. This is how I'm going to go. Eaten by a grizzly bear.*

The bear was still headed our way, running now. Water splashed twice as high as the bear as his enormous paws thundered through the river. He let out a massive roar that turned my insides to liquid. I was frozen in fear, tears suddenly streaming down my cheeks. Only a few feet away now, the grizzly reared up onto its hind legs and lunged into the air straight toward me.

But instead of landing on top of me, he caught a salmon in mid-air. He dropped back onto the bank of the river directly in front of us and proceeded to rip it to shreds right before our eyes. I blinked. Suddenly, the intense panic was gone. This grizzly wasn't after us. He was after a fish dinner.

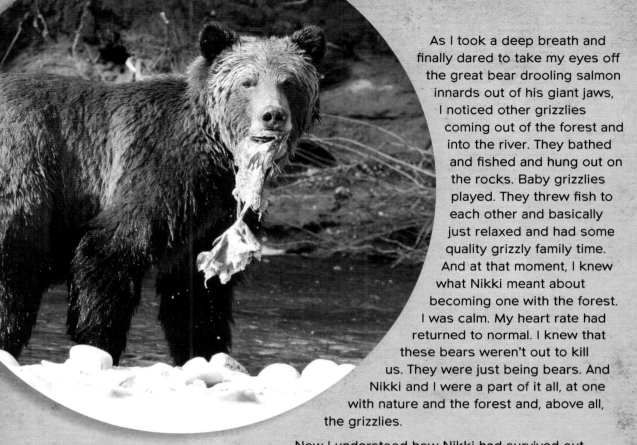

As I took a deep breath and finally dared to take my eyes off the great bear drooling salmon innards out of his giant jaws, I noticed other grizzlies coming out of the forest and into the river. They bathed and fished and hung out on the rocks. Baby grizzlies played. They threw fish to each other and basically just relaxed and had some quality grizzly family time. And at that moment, I knew what Nikki meant about becoming one with the forest. I was calm. My heart rate had returned to normal. I knew that these bears weren't out to kill us. They were just being bears. And Nikki and I were a part of it all, at one with nature and the forest and, above all, the grizzlies.

Now I understood how Nikki had survived out here all of this time. Sometimes we can get disconnected from nature, and we tend to fear the unfamiliar rather than appreciate it. It's important to let your heart be wild and let yourself live with the same spirit as nature. My papa always told me, when you cage a wild animal, tame it, and release it back into the wild, what happens to it? It dies. What my parents taught me and what Nikki and the grizzlies reminded me is that it's always important to keep a little bit of that wild in you.

spirit bears

kermode or spirit bears (*Ursus americanus kermodei*) are a subspecies of North American black bears easily recognized by their all-white or cream-colored fur. A recessive gene gives them their distinctive appearance, but they still have pigment in their eyes and skin. This means spirit bears are not considered albino. About 400 individuals live in the Great Bear Rainforest, where they are protected as sacred by local indigenous or First Nations communities.

As my time with Nikki and the grizzlies came to an end, I was excited to get back to the sharks in the sea, but I was forever grateful for this life-changing experience. Facing my greatest fear was a very humbling experience, and the anxieties that I felt put me very much outside of my comfort zone. But I think that's when we grow the most—when we face our fears and are stronger for it.

And being in touch with nature, taking a moment to really see the world around us, helps us grow, too. You don't have to survive naked on an island for a month or live with grizzly bears to have a wild adventure. Any moment spent outdoors, whether camping, watching wildlife, or trying local fresh foods, can harness a bit of the wild fuel we need to go after our dreams, face our fears, and not only survive, but thrive.

PHOTO CREDITS